The Women Chefs
of Britain

The Women Chefs of Britain

A wonderful collection of recipes
from the leading women chefs
of the British Isles

Joanne Wickens.

ABSOLUTE PRESS

First published in 1990 by Absolute Press
Scarborough House, 29 James Street West, Bath, England

This edition first published November 1995

© Absolute Press 1995

ISBN 0 948230 84 3

Editor: Nicki Morris
Cover and text design: Humphrey Stone
Cover photograph © Anthony Blake Library
Phototypeset by Character Graphics, Taunton
Printed by Longdunn Press Ltd, Bristol

ISBN 0 948230 34 7

Contents

Introduction

Take fifty-seven women chefs. Each working long, hard hours, often single-handed, some with a husband or partner – none with a 'brigade de cuisine'. Ask each one for recipes for a three-course dinner party menu which epitomises their own style of cooking. Stand back and wait for the explosion … but the explosion was one of delight and enthusiasm. Instead of protests about adding to their already huge workload, there was a positive flood of imaginative ideas and suggestions – even a hint of friendly rivalry. A wide variety of different establishments is represented here – from grand country house hotels like Ballymaloe in County Cork to the more streamlined restaurants like Clarke's in Kensington. But as the recipes started to trickle in, an unmistakable common theme began to appear – unlike many chefs' recipes, these were all eminently 'cookable' and demonstrated a love and respect for fresh, natural ingredients. This book is a celebration of the ever-growing number of women chefs – the incredibly high standards you will find in their restaurants are reflected in these recipes.

Betty Allen

THE AIRDS HOTEL · PORT APPIN

*When we bought the Airds Hotel in 1978, supplies presented the greatest
difficulty. No one delivered and we had to drive an hour each way to Oban,
twice weekly, to collect every single item we required. Now, twelve years
later, there are many improvements and everything is delivered, some items
by a combination of rail and taxi. The only person who does not deliver is our
fishmonger in Oban who sends our fish by bus; the driver deposits the parcel
at a stop on the main road. We drive about two miles along our single-track
road to collect it. This system works well apart from one day when the fish
was not to be found. Mr Binnie informed us over the telephone
that the fish had missed the bus!*

MOUSSELINE OF SCALLOPS WITH CHAMPAGNE AND CHIVE SAUCE

Serves 6 – 8

*12 oz (350g) scallops
salt to taste
pinch cayenne pepper
8 oz (225g) sole (skinned weight)
18 fl oz (500ml) double cream*

FOR THE CHAMPAGNE AND CHIVE SAUCE

*1 shallot, finely chopped
a little butter
½ pint (275ml) champagne
½ pint (275ml) fish stock
½ pint (275ml) double cream
small bunch chives, finely chopped*

Remove corals and dry the scallops. Finely mince the scallops and sole, then pass the mixture through a sieve, keeping both bowls on ice. Leave in a refrigerator for 4 hours. Gradually whisk in the cream, using an electric beater. Season.

Brush 10 ramekins or small moulds with melted butter and pour in the mixture, tapping lightly to get rid of any air bubbles. Pre-heat the oven to 300°F/150°C/Gas 2 and poach the mousselines in a bain-marie of warm water for 20–25 minutes.

To make the sauce, soften the shallot in the butter, then add the champagne and fish stock and reduce till syrupy. Add the cream and reduce to the desired thickness. Add the finely chopped chives and season before serving.

When the centre of the mousseline is just firm, remove from the oven and leave for 5–10 minutes before turning out. Place on a warm plate and serve with the champagne and chive sauce.

BREAST OF PHEASANT WITH A WHISKY AND GRAPE SAUCE

Serves 4

2 shallots or ½ small onion, finely chopped
butter for frying
5 fl oz (150ml) red wine
5 fl oz (150ml) good chicken stock
2–3 tablespoons whisky
4 boned pheasant breasts, skin removed
5 fl oz (150ml) double cream
4 oz (125g) black grapes, halved and seeded

Soften the shallots in a little butter. Add the wine, stock and whisky and boil down to 2 or 3 tablespoons.

Heat a little butter in a large non-stick pan and brown the pheasant breasts on both sides. Turn down the heat and continue to cook for about 5–7 minutes each side.

Add any cooking juices together with the cream to the sauce. Bring to boiling point, add the grapes, check for seasoning and simmer for 2 minutes more. Slice each breast into 3 and arrange on hot plates with the sauce poured around.

ORANGE AND GRAND MARNIER TERRINE

Serves 6 – 8

½ oz (10g) gelatine
½ pint (275ml) water
8 oz (225g) sugar
11 oranges
1½ tablespoons Grand Marnier

Soak the gelatine in a little of the water in a bowl set over a pan of warm water. Warm the remainder of the water with the sugar and the zest of 1 of the oranges until the sugar has dissolved. Allow to cool a little then stir in the dissolved gelatine.

Finely slice the peel of 2 of the oranges and immerse in boiling water for 20 seconds. Drain and leave to cool. Peel and segment all the oranges.

Cut pieces of bakewell paper to fit the bottom of 2 loaf tins, making it long enough to overlap the top ends of the tins. Dampen the tins and paper with water. Strain the syrup through a fine sieve and add the Grand Marnier.

Carefully layer the syrup and oranges and rind into the tins, trying to let each layer set a little before adding more. Try to set the oranges into the syrup rather than making definite layers which cause the jelly to break up when cutting later.

Refrigerate for several hours. Gently ease out of the tin and slice.

Myrtle Allen

BALLYMALOE HOUSE · SHANAGARRY
COUNTY CORK

Ever since we placed our first advertisement in the Cork Examiner in 1964, 'Dine in a Country House', it has been our endeavour to emulate the food of the best country houses in Ireland. To this end we have always gone down to our own garden and glass houses, into our local butcher's shop and to the pier at Ballycotton to collect our produce. We write a new menu each afternoon when we see what we have got. Mr Cuddigan, our butcher, watches over his cattle and sheep down to the last sprig of burnet in his old pastures and the sweet meadow grasses in his hay. Patty Walshe rears pigs for us in a non-intensive way and neighbouring farmers' wives bring us their beautiful poultry. Our cheeseboard celebrates the remarkable rebirth of Irish cheeses from small farms all over the country; we especially welcome Breda Coogan's cheese, the newest arrival, and Tim O'Connell of the Mitchelstown Co-operative group who consistently keeps us supplied with Irish 'Cheddar' in large cloth-bound rolls.

CHICKEN LIVER PÂTÉ

Serves 6

4 oz (125g) Irish salted butter
4 oz (125g) chicken livers
2 tablespoons brandy
1 clove garlic
1 teaspoon thyme leaves
few grinds pepper and salt to taste

FOR THE TOMATO CONCASSE

1 lb (450g) tomatoes
salt, pepper and sugar to taste
2½ fl oz (60ml) French dressing
fresh basil leaves

Warm 2 oz (50g) of the butter until foaming. Add the chicken livers and fry gently, turning occasionally until just cooked through. Put the livers and butter through a sieve or blender to make a smooth paste. Deglaze the pan with the brandy, scraping up all the sticky residue. Add this liquid to the livers along with the garlic. Blend or sieve again and allow to cool.

Soften the remaining butter and beat it in, then add the thyme leaves and pepper and taste for seasoning. Pack into a rectangular ½ lb (225g) loaf tin, press clingfilm down close to the top to make a tight seal and refrigerate until firmly set.

Just before serving, prepare the tomato concasse. Scald, peel and deseed the tomatoes. Cut the flesh into ¼ inch (0.5cm) dice and sprinkle with small pinch of salt and sugar and a good grinding of black pepper. Toss in French dressing and sprinkle with the basil.

To serve, cut ¼ inch (0.5cm) slices of the pâté in half diagonally. Place some of the tomato concasse between the two halves and accompany with toast or crispy bread. Once cut, do not leave the pâté exposed to the air as its appearance and flavour will alter.

BAKED BASS WITH SPINACH SAUCE

Serves 3

2 lb (900g) bass
1–2oz (25–50g) butter
salt and pepper
1 sprig fennel

FOR THE SAUCE

8 fl oz (225ml) cream
5 oz (150g) butter
4 oz (125g) spinach leaves

Season the fish and dot with butter and fennel. Wrap in tin foil, folding carefully so that no butter can escape during the cooking. Bake for approximately 30 minutes at 375°F/190°C/Gas 5. Unwrap and place the fish on a heated serving dish.

Meanwhile make the sauce. Boil the cream down to about 3 tablespoonfuls, taking care that it does not burn or turn yellow. Beat in the butter bit by bit as for Hollandaise sauce. Meanwhile boil about 1 pint (570ml) water, adding salt only if using unsalted butter. Cook the spinach leaves in this for 5 minutes. Remove, drain and chop roughly into 1 inch (2.5cm) pieces and stir into the sauce along with the cooking juices from the fish.

RASPBERRY ICE CREAM

Serves 6

1 lb (450g) raspberries
10 oz (275g) sugar
1 teaspoon gelatine
1 pint (570ml) whipped cream

Make the raspberry purée by rubbing the raw fruit through a sieve or spinning in a food processor. The pips may be strained out. You will need 14 fl oz (375ml) of purée.

Dissolve the sugar in 5 fl oz (150ml) water and boil for 1 minute. Soften the gelatine in 1 tablespoon water and heat over a saucepan of boiling water until completely dissolved.

Gradually blend the raspberry purée with the sugar and water syrup and gelatine. When cool, fold in the whipped cream and set to freeze; we do not usually make this in a machine. Remove from the freezer 10 – 15 minutes before serving to soften a little.

Mary Alley

WOODS · BATH

I have been cooking at Woods for ten years now. The emphasis in our menu is on healthy eating – everything is homemade on the premises and use of butter, cream and flour is limited. Best quality basic ingredients are the most important thing in my cooking and we are lucky in having some excellent suppliers – Wing Fish of St Mawes in Cornwall bring wonderful fresh fish to Bath twice a week; meat, which we bone and hang ourselves, is from Birmingham market; and Vin Sullivan of Abergavenny supplies a wide range of produce.

RARE ROAST BEEF FILLET WITH STEM GINGER AND ARMAGNAC JELLY

Serves 4

10 oz (275g) beef fillet, all fat removed and well seasoned with coarse black pepper
olive oil

FOR THE GINGER AND ARMAGNAC JELLY

1 piece stem ginger, finely chopped
8 fl oz (225ml) red wine
½ cup brown sugar
4 fl oz (125ml) red wine vinegar
1 measure Armagnac
1 measure port
2 leaves gelatine, softened in cold water

Heat the olive oil in a frying pan, seal the meat all over and place in a hot oven for 8 minutes. Remove and leave to rest in a cool place (not a fridge).

Mix together all the ingredients for the jelly, except the gelatine. Reduce by half, then add the gelatine and stir until dissolved. Set over ice, stirring occasionally so that the ginger is evenly distributed.

When the jelly is set, roughly chop, and serve 2 or 3 slices of the beef fillet surrounded by jelly.

BREAST OF CHICKEN MARINATED WITH TAMARI, GREEN CHILLIS, GINGER AND FRESH CORIANDER

Serves 4

FOR THE MARINADE

2½ level dessertspoons freshly chopped coriander
1 inch (2.5cm) piece ginger,
peeled and finely chopped
2 garlic cloves
3 fl oz (75ml) brown rice vinegar
rind and juice of 2 lemons
1 dessertspoon honey
1 green chilli, deseeded and finely chopped
4 fl oz (125ml) tamari
½ cup olive oil
½ cup walnut oil
2 fl oz (50ml) white wine
1 tablespoon hot chilli oil

4 chicken breasts, skinned and wing piece removed

Combine all the ingredients for the marinade and add the chicken. Marinate for at least 6–8 hours. Then roast for approximately 20 minutes in a moderate oven, basting with the marinade every 10 minutes. Serve with sauté potatoes or rice.

CHOCOLATE ROULADE

Serves 4

2 large free range eggs
3½ oz (100g) warmed caster sugar
1½ oz (40g) plain flour
½ oz (10g) cocoa powder
¼ oz (5g) glycerine

chocolate and orange mousse or cream with
fresh fruit, to fill
fresh apricot purée, to serve.

Whisk the eggs until very light and fluffy. Add the warmed suggar and continue whisking until it reaches the ribbon stage. Then fold in the sieved flour and cocoa powder and finally the glycerine.

Spread evenly on to a piece of flat waxed paper and bake in a moderate oven until just cooked – about 7 minutes.

Remove from the oven and put the sponge side down on to another piece of lightly dusted waxed paper; take off the top piece of paper very gently. Cool, trim and cut in half. Lay one half inside the curved semi-circle of a jam roly-poly tin. Fill with either chocolate and orange mousse or, if you prefer, just cream with strawberries or bananas and lay the second piece of sponge flat on top. Cover very tightly with cling film and chill for 1–2 hours before serving on a fresh apricot purée.

Sue Blockey

Tiroran is a remote and enchanting sporting lodge nestling against the hills and forests on the shores of Loch Scridain. We fell in love with it thirteen years ago, and it is very much our home. During the summer months we open as a small country house hotel, and take up to seventeen guests. Fish, venison, beef and lamb all come from the island; and together with our own soft fruits, salads, herbs and eggs from our own hens and ducks, enable us to serve good wholesome fresh food.

SMOKED MUSSEL CROUSTADES WITH A LEMON BUTTER SAUCE

Serves 6

4–5 smoked mussels per person
flour
pinhead oatmeal
butter
6 rounds of stale bread, about 2/3 inch thick
oil

FOR THE SAUCE

2 egg yolks
1 tablespoon lemon juice
3 oz (75g) melted butter
3 tablespoons double cream
salt and pepper
paprika, lemon slices and fresh fennel, to decorate

We are lucky on Mull to have a marvellous supply of lovely plump mussels which are locally smoked, but a good brand of tinned ones will do very well – drain the oil before using.

Toss the mussels in an equal mixture of flour and pinhead oatmeal. Sauté lightly in butter for 1–2 minutes and keep warm. Fry the rounds of bread in hot oil until a light golden brown. Drain. Place 4–5 mussels on each round of bread and keep warm.

To make the sauce, put the egg yolks and lemon juice in a bowl set over hot water. Gradually whisk in the melted butter until very thick. Stir in the cream and season to taste. Cover the bowl and leave over hot water with the heat turned off. Just before serving, pour over the mussels, dust with paprika and a little finely snipped fresh fennel. Decorate with a twist of lemon and a small sprig of fennel.

LOIN OF SCOTCH LAMB WITH PLUM SAUCE

Serves 6

3 lbs (1.4kg) loin of Scotch lamb (with kidney),
boned
1 tablespoon oil
2 oz (50g) bacon, finely chopped
1 bunch watercress, washed and finely chopped
2 oz (50g) walnut pieces
4 oz (125g) cooked long grain rice
3 level tablespoons coarse grain mustard
1 egg, beaten
salt and pepper
1 lb (450g) red plums
½ pint (275ml) red wine
dark brown sugar

The local lamb has a wonderful flavour. The sheep graze the heather and also the sea-washed shore grass and the seaweed, giving the meat a slight gamey flavour not unlike the French agneau de Pré-sales (the sheep which graze on the salty grasses of the Normandy coast). We like our lamb to be pink and juicy – it seems a shame to turn the meat grey with over cooking.

Skin, core and chop the kidney finely. Sauté in the oil with the bacon. Take the pan off the heat and stir in the watercress, chopped nuts and rice, 1 tablespoon of the mustard, the beaten egg and seasoning.

Open up the lamb and spoon the stuffing along the length of the meat. Fold the meat over the stuffing and secure with string. Score deep lines across the fat and work the remaining mustard well down into the cuts, which will give the joint a good crispy crust. Roast at 425°F/220°C/Gas 7 for just about 1¼ hours. Keep warm. Skim and reserve the juices.

Poach the plums in the wine until just tender, reserving a few for garnishing. Drain and reserve the juice. Purée the plums and their juice along with the reserved roasting juices. Sweeten to taste with a little dark brown sugar. Garnish with whole plums and watercress sprigs.

PEPPERED STRAWBERRIES WITH ORANGE SHORTBREAD

Serves 6

2 lbs (900g) firm, ripe strawberries
3 inch cinnamon stick
12 black peppercorns, roughly chopped
5 oz (150g) granulated sugar
¾ bottle Beaujolais

FOR THE SHORTBREAD

8 oz (225g) butter
1 cup icing sugar
1 cup cornflour
2 cups soft plain flour
grated zest of half an orange
caster sugar

Hull the strawberries and put them in a large serving bowl. Heat the remaining ingredients together gently and when the sugar has dissolved, bring the wine to the boil and allow to boil for 7 minutes or so to reduce by about a third. Cool, then sieve over the strawberries. Serve chilled.

To make the shortbread, cream together the butter and icing sugar. Mix in the sifted flours and grated zest. Knead gently. Grease a 10 inch (25cm) loose bottomed flan dish and pack in the mixture. Smooth the surface and leave in the fridge for ½ hour. Prick the surface all over with a fork. Bake at 300°F/150°C/Gas 2 for 30–40 minutes. Then dust lightly with caster sugar and give 7 minutes more in a very cool oven. Cut while still warm.

Tessa Bramley

OLD VICARAGE · RIDGEWAY MOOR

The meal we have chosen is from a typical springtime menu at the Old Vicarage. In the restaurant we would start with an amuse-gueule *of some raw wild salmon made into a tartare with some dill and served with a hazelnut oil dressed salad of herbs and tiny salad shoots. The langoustine dish looks spectacular, but tastes better: heady and sweet, with the rich scents of saffron and thyme. For the main course the ducks should be free range, with a good, firm pink-tinged flesh. Ours come from a farm in Ridgeway village, where they are left to wander about the yard. The flavour and texture of the dish is enhanced if you can leave the meat still slightly pink when it is cooked. There is still a nip in the air at night at this time of year so a wicked chocolate pudding is good to end the dinner – light in texture but with a very concentrated flavour. It is our most popular pudding; in fact our customers never allow us to take it off the menu!*

MILLE-FEUILLES OF LANGOUSTINES WITH A SAFFRON BUTTER SAUCE

Serves 4

FOR THE SAUCE
*mirepoix of 1 small onion, 2 sticks celery,
white part of 1 leek
2 oz (50g) butter
langoustine shells
2 tablespoons white wine vinegar
1 tablespoon brandy
½ pint (275ml) cream, infused
with 1 pinch saffron stamens
small bunch thyme
1 sprig dill
seasoning
1 teaspoon tomato purée*

*4 sheets filo pastry
melted unsalted butter, for brushing
24 large live langoustines, shells removed
and tails deveined
butter for frying
sprigs of thyme, for garnishing
courgette and pepper brunois, for serving*

Sweat the mirepoix in 1 oz (25g) butter. Cook the langoustine shells quickly over a high heat in 1 oz (25g) butter until they turn pink and give off a good fresh sea smell. Add the tomato purée. Add the mirepoix, then the white wine vinegar and reduce. Add the brandy and reduce again. Add the saffron and cream infusion and herbs, then reduce until the sauce has thickened and the flavours have amalgamated. Season and press through a fine sieve, pressing out the juices from the residue. Check seasoning again.

Brush 1 sheet of filo with melted butter. Lay a

second sheet on top and brush again; repeat with the remaining sheets. With a round 3 inch (7.5cm) cutter, cut out 12 circles. Bake on a greased baking sheet in a preheated oven 400°F/200°C/Gas 6 for 4–5 minutes until crisp, puffy and golden.

Fry the langoustine tails in butter, taking care to turn them and cook gently so that they do not toughen. Season but do not use black pepper as this spoils the appearance.

On each heated serving plate, layer 3 filo circles with langoustine tails between each layer. Place a tiny sprig of thyme on the top circle and pour the sauce around. Garnish with tiny piles of courgette and pepper brunois.

SALMI OF DUCK WITH BRAISED LEEKS AND HAM

Serves 4

2 ducks, approx 4 lbs (1.8kg)
2 leeks, each cut into 8 pieces
mirepoix of 1 stick celery, 1 carrot, 6 shallots
4 mushrooms, quartered
1 oz (25g) butter
½ glass full-bodied red wine eg. Rioja
1 sherry glass Madeira
3 sprigs sage
2 sprigs summer savory
2 cloves
6 peppercorns
1 slice lean ham, cut into batons

Remove the breasts and legs from the ducks and reserve, together with the livers. Use the carcase and giblets to make 1 pint (570ml) stock. Skin the legs and cook, covered with the ham, in the stock for 45 minutes in a preheated oven (400°F/200°C/Gas 6). Roast the breasts for the last 8–10 minutes of cooking time until pink. Put the legs and breasts to one side.

Braise the leeks in a little stock and butter until softened; keep warm, Fry the mirepoix and mushrooms in butter until well browned. Add the red wine and reduce to a syrup. Add the Madeira, herbs and spices and reduce again. Add the cooking liquor from the braised legs. Put the duck legs into the sauce and continue cooking on top of the stove. Skin the breasts and add these to the pan. Heat gently until the breasts are cooked but still slightly pink and the leg meat leaves the bone easily. Taste and adjust the seasoning. The sauce should be full in flavour, thick and syrupy.

In a separate pan, lightly sauté the duck livers. Serve the duck meat and livers with the sauce poured around and the braised leeks as a bright garnish.

BAKED CHOCOLATE PUDDING WITH FUDGE SAUCE AND CUSTARD

Serves 4

3½ oz (75g) self-raising flour
¾ level teaspoon bicarbonate of soda
½ level teaspoon baking powder
1 tablespoon cocoa
2½ oz (65g) caster sugar
1 large egg
1 tablespoon golden syrup
3½ fl oz (100ml) milk
3½ fl oz (100ml) sunflower oil

FOR THE FUDGE SAUCE

1 oz (25g) unsalted butter
3 oz (75g) unsweetened
bitter chocolate (the purest possible)
7 fl oz (200ml) cream
8 oz (225g) icing sugar
homemade custard (Crème Anglaise) to serve

Sieve all the dry ingredients twice. Make a well in the centre and drop in the egg, golden syrup and the milk and oil mixed. Mix together to make a batter.

Grease 4 x 6 fl oz (175ml) pudding tins and pour in the mixture. Bake in a preheated oven (275°F/140°C/Gas 1) for 30–35 minutes until the puddings are springy to the touch.

To make the fudge sauce, bring the butter, chocolate and cream slowly to the boil in a double boiler. Remove from the heat and gradually beat in the icing sugar until smooth and glossy.

To serve, pour the fudge over the puddings and serve with a good custard made with free range eggs and a vanilla pod.

Hilary Brown

LA POTINIÈRE, · GULLANE

We open for lunch four times a week and dinner twice. We bought the restaurant after lunching here in 1975 – despite having no previous experience! 'La Potinière' means 'the gossiping place' and encapsulates both French and Scottish influences which are echoed in my approach to cooking. We run the restaurant on our own and make a point of seeking out fresh produce ourselves, basing the day's menu on the best ingredients available. We offer a fixed menu and because many of our customers are regulars, we always keep a record so that we can vary it for them as much as possible.

Recipes from 'La Potinière and Friends' by David and Hilary Brown, Century £16.99.

TOMATO AND MINT SOUP

Serves 6

2 oz (50g) unsalted butter
8 oz (225g) onions, peeled and finely sliced
2 lb (900g) tomatoes (the redder the better)
3 fl oz (75ml) dry sherry
1 tablespoon caster sugar
1½ rounded tablespoons dried mint or
3 rounded tablespoons chopped fresh mint
seasoning
sprigs of fresh mint, plus lightly whipped cream, to garnish

Melt the butter in a medium-sized saucepan. Add the onion and cook gently until softened but not coloured. Stir from time to time with a wooden spoon. Add the tomatoes whole, with skins and stalks, the sherry, sugar and mint. No water is required at this stage. Stir together, cover with a lid, then simmer for 45 minutes. Stir occasionally. Ladle the mixture into a liquidiser and blend until smooth.

Pour the soup through a mouli into the rinsed out pan. Stir together, then add enough water to correct the consistency. Season to taste, about 1–2 teaspoons salt. It should have plenty of body so do not add too much water. The tomatoes should have created enough liquid.

Reheat the soup when wishing to serve and ladle into warmed soup bowls or one large tureen. Garnish with a little lightly whipped cream, topped with a sprig of fresh mint.

[19]

PIGEON BREAST WITH LENTILS AND MOREL SAUCE

Serves 6

6 fresh wood pigeons
1 dessertspoon each hazelnut and
olive oils
4 oz (125g) brown lentils, soaked for 1 hour
in warm water with a slice of onion
2½ fl oz (65ml) strong pigeon stock
1 tablespoon chopped fresh tarragon
or 1 teaspoon dried
1 oz (25g) unsalted butter
seasoning

FOR THE MOREL SAUCE

5 fl oz (150ml) dry white wine
5 fl oz (150ml) strong pigeon stock
5 fl oz (150ml) double cream
½ oz (10g) dried morels,
soaked for 1 hour in warm water

Using a small sharp knife, carefully cut away each breast, keeping your knife as close to the rib cage as possible. Pull off the skin and then place the breasts in a bowl. Pour the oils over them and mix well so that every surface is coated. Cover and set aside in a cool place. I normally prepare them the evening before and refrigerate them overnight. The next day, allow them to come to room temperature before cooking.

Prepare the sauce by placing the wine in a small to medium pan, bringing to the boil, and simmering until reduced by half. Add the stock and once again bring to the boil and simmer until reduced by half. Add the cream, move the pan half on, half off the burner or hot plate, and allow to simmer until a smooth sauce-like consistency is reached.

Squeeze most of the water out of the morels and add them to the sauce. Set aside until needed, during which time the flavour of the morels will penetrate the sauce. Preheat the oven to 450°F/230°C/Gas 8.

Pour the lentils through a sieve, and place in a pan along with the slice of onion. Cover with cold water, bring to the boil and simmer for 2 minutes. Pour through a sieve, remove the onion, and return to the pan. Add the stock, the tarragon and half of the butter. Season with a little salt and freshly ground black pepper.

Melt the remaining butter in a large frying pan and, when hot, add the breasts. Season lightly with salt, then turn over using tongs. Once they have been browned on both sides, place on a lightly buttered baking tray. You may have to brown them in two batches, depending on the size of your frying pan. Place on the middle shelf in the preheated oven for 7 or 8 minutes, depending on their size.

During this time, reheat the lentils and simmer for about 5 minutes by which time they should be softened, but still whole and not in any way mushy. Add a little water if the lentils are too dry, and stir with a wooden spoon to make sure that they are not sticking. Check for temperature and seasoning and adjust if necessary.

Reheat the sauce gently. Taste for seasoning, but I normally find that the flavour is intense enough without needing to add any salt. Remove the pigeons and allow to rest in a warm place for at least 5 minutes, which ensures that they will be evenly rosy inside.

To serve, place a spoonful of lentils on each heated serving plate. Spoon the sauce around the lentils, making sure that everyone gets their share of the morels. Place the breasts on a chopping board and cut across, at an angle, into four slices. Arrange eight of these on each mound of lentils, and serve immediately.

ICED ORANGE SOUFFLÉ

Serves 16 – 18

4 x size 2 eggs
5 oz (150g) caster sugar
finely grated rind and juice of 2 small oranges
2 tablespoons Cointreau
1 pint (570ml) double cream, chilled
5-6 oz (150-175g) almond ratafia biscuits,
crushed to a powder in a food processor

FOR THE CARAMEL SAUCE

8 oz (225g) caster sugar
strips of orange peel
4-5 navel oranges, to decorate

Make the caramel sauce first so that it has time to cool. In a heavy pan or frying pan, let the caster sugar melt over a moderate heat. Stir now and again to make sure that it melts evenly. When it has turned a deep golden or chestnut colour, add 5 fl oz (150ml) hot water. Remember that the caramel will continue to darken until the water is added, so have it ready. Be careful as the combination will produce sparks of very hot caramel. Either use a long-handled spoon to stir the hot caramel, or wear rubber gloves. Stir over a moderate heat until the caramel and water mix thoroughly and a smooth sauce is formed. Let it boil for a few minutes until it thickens slightly. The diameter of the pan determines how long this will take, as the wider the pan, the quicker the water will evaporate. Pour into a bowl. It will thicken more as it cools.

While it is cooling, cut some julienne strips of orange peel. Rinse and dry one of your decoration oranges. Using a sharp fine knife, cut very, very thin strips, about ¾ in (2cm) wide, down the length of the orange. Place these on a chopping board and cut into thin strips. Place in a small pan of cold water, bring to the boil and boil for 5 minutes. Pour through a sieve, run plenty of cold water over them to remove their bitter taste, shake dry and add to the cooling caramel sauce.

Separate the eggs, being very careful that no egg yolk, not even a speck, goes into the whites. (This applies any time you are going to be whisking them). Place the yolks in the bowl of a free-standing mixer, if using one, and the whites in another bowl. Both should be fairly big to allow room for expansion.

Start whisking the yolks, gradually adding the sugar, a tablespoon or so at a time. This ensures as light a mixture as possible. Continue to whisk while adding the orange juice and rind, and carry on until the mixture is very pale and thick, and has increased in volume. Add the Cointreau at the last minute and switch off when mixed in.

If your hands are free, while this is whisking, beat the cream in yet another bowl until it will form soft trails if dropped from lifted beaters. (Be careful when beating the cream that flying cream doesn't go into the bowl of egg whites, as anything fatty spoils their whisking qualities.) Wash the beaters thoroughly, dry them, then whisk the whites until they will form little peaks when the surface is dabbed with the beaters.

Using a spatula, empty the cream on to the orange mousse mixture, and using a balloon whisk or large metal spoon, fold together. Add a spoonful or two of the whisked white, beat in fairly roughly, then very gently fold in the remainder using a large metal spoon. At this stage the mixture should start to thicken. Stop as soon as the ingredients are thoroughly mixed.

Sprinkle 2 tablespoons of crushed ratafias evenly along each base of two loaf tins of 1¾-2 pint (1-1.2 litre) capacity. Ladle the soufflé into them, being careful not to disturb the crumbs. Gently level the top with the back of a spoon or a palette knife, then sieve the remaining crushed ratafias over the surfaces. Pat down gently, then transfer to your freezer straightaway. Freeze for at least 4 hours. I generally make mine the day before (or should I say in the wee small hours, as very often I start some preparation for the next day once we have cleared up the restaurant after serving dinner on a Saturday or after a private party, at about 1am).

Allow the soufflé to soften before serving. How long this takes depends on how long it has been frozen, and the temperature of your kitchen. If it has had 4 hours only, 10 minutes should be long enough, but if it has been frozen overnight or longer, remove it from the freezer 45 minutes before you wish to serve it. I prefer to serve the slices of soufflé when they are rather soft and mousse-like, but you may prefer them to be fairly hard.

While the soufflé is softening, prepare the oranges by cutting away the skin and pith. Using a sharp knife, cut off the top, then using a sawing motion, and turning the orange round in one hand, peel away the skin and pith in one long strip. Alternatively cut off the top and the bottom, sit it on a chopping board, and cut downwards in inch-wide (2.5cm) strips, cutting between the flesh and the pith. Cut the oranges in half lengthwise, then across into $\frac{1}{4}$ in (6mm) slices.

Turn the soufflé out on to a flat plate or board, by running a knife round the edge of it, right down to the base of the tin. Turn upside down and if it does not come out immediately, grasp both the tin and the board and give them a sharp jolt. Trim off the very outside edge, then cut into $\frac{1}{2}$-$\frac{3}{4}$ in (1-2cm) slices, allowing the slices to fall on to a fish slice as you cut them, Transfer on to a serving plate, on the fish slice. Repeat with the other slices. Place two or three pieces of orange on the plate, to the underside of the slice, coat with a tablespoon of caramel sauce and serve immediately.

Susan Campion

I always say that we live in a field in Kent. Actually the Auberge is in the middle of three acres and very secluded. We have to send precise directions to all our visitors. The first person I met when we moved in was 'Lorna the milk'. Without her we would all fall apart. As well as milk and cream she delivers the newspapers, her own free range chicken, duck and goose eggs – the ducks and geese themselves, turkeys at Christmas, all our soft fruit in summer, vegetables; in fact she grows or rears almost everything – organically, too. She also delivers all the local gossip and has just been awarded the B.E.M. (but not for that). However, she has not up to now come up with any lamb, so we get our Romney Marsh lamb from Ron Cooper, our local butcher at Bradbourne Lees, who incidentally supplies the Connaught Hotel and also has marvellous beef, pork and game.

SCALLOP AND LEEK TARTS

Serves 4

3 oz (75g) self-raising wholemeal flour
3 oz (75g) plain unbleached white flour
½ oz (10g) icing sugar
pinch salt
4 oz (125g) butter, cut into pieces
cold water

FOR THE FILLING

4 scallops
3 oz (75g) butter
3 small leeks (washed, dried and finely shredded)
1 oz (25g) plain white flour
½ pint (275ml) good fish stock mixed with dry
white wine
1 egg yolk
2 fl oz (50ml) double cream
chopped parsley or chervil

2 oz (50g) Gruyère, grated
fresh ground salt and pepper

These Scallop and Leek tarts were the first dish I served when we opened the Auberge. I felt we should start with something completely new. Scallops were in season and we bought them as we still do with all our other fish – from Mr Griggs whose shop is on the beach at Hythe.

Sift together the flours, icing sugar and salt and put into a food processor with the butter. Whiz until only coarsely crumbed. Add just enough cold water to form a lump. Knead briefly, wrap in clingfilm and chill for at least an hour.

Roll out the pastry and line 4 x 4 inch (10cm) tart tins; replace in the refrigerator for ½ hour. Prick the bottoms and bake blind for 20 minutes at 375°F/190°C/Gas 5 until lightly browned.

Cut the scallops in two horizontally, leaving the corals whole. Wash and pat dry. Sauté briefly in 1 oz (25g) of the butter, then put to one side. Soften the shredded leeks in 1 oz (25g) of the butter; put them to one side as well.

Melt the remaining 1 oz (25g) of butter in a small pan – stir in the flour and cook for 1 minute over a low heat; then add the warmed wine and stock mixture, stirring briskly to make a smooth sauce. Simmer gently for 10 minutes, stirring occasionally.

Meanwhile divide the leeks between the 4 cooked pastry cases and arrange the scallops on top with a circle of the coral on each side.

Beat the egg yolk and cream together and add to the sauce, stirring all the time. Heat gently without allowing to boil (or it will curdle). Add salt and pepper to taste and the chopped parsley or chervil. Cover the leeks and scallops with this sauce, sprinkle on the grated Gruyère and place in a preheated oven at 350°F/180°C/Gas 4 for about 10 minutes until the cheese has melted. Serve at once with a small radicchio and Belgian endive salad dressed with a hazelnut or walnut oil and lemon juice dressing.

ROAST RACK OF LAMB WITH A CONFIT OF SMALL ONIONS AND GARLIC

Serves 4

FOR THE COATING
1 tablespoon freshly grated
Parmesan cheese
1 tablespoon Dijon mustard
2 oz (50g) mixed olive oil and melted butter
fresh ground salt and pepper
3 tablespoons fine fresh breadcrumbs

*2 whole best ends of lamb – French trimmed**

FOR THE CONFIT
16 small pickling onions
12 large cloves garlic
2 oz (50g) butter
1 tablespoon olive oil
2 tablespoons dark brown sugar
1 glass red wine
2 oz (50g) sultanas
fresh ground salt and pepper
2 tablespoons jellied stock
watercress for garnish

An hour before cooking, mix all the ingredients for the coating together and coat the meat with the mixture. When the meat has rested, roast at the top of a very hot oven 450°F/230°C/Gas 8 for 20 minutes (medium rare).

The confit can be made well ahead. Blanch the unpeeled onions and garlic for 2 minutes. Strain, refresh and peel. Melt the oil and butter together, add the whole onions and garlic and stir until they are well coated. Stir in the sugar, cover the pan and simmer gently for about ½ hour without allowing to burn.

Add the red wine, sultanas and seasoning. Cover and simmer until the onions and garlic are very tender but not falling apart. When ready to serve, just stir in the jellied stock and reheat.

To serve, carve the lamb into chops, carefully spoon the confit beside each portion and decorate with watercress. I serve this with a gratin of courgettes and chives.

*A good butcher should do this if asked. Saw across the rib bones leaving approx. 3 inches (7.5cm). Remove the meat from between the bones (stopping of course at the main chop meat so that the ribs stick up like fingers). Chine the back bone and remove, together with the piece of white gristle that runs along the base. This is called 'French trimmed'.

FROZEN PRALINE SOUFFLÉ WITH MOCCHA SAUCE

Serves 4

3 oz (75g) granulated sugar
3 oz (75g) unblanched almonds
½ pint (275ml) double cream
2 tablespoons Tia Maria
2 egg whites
pinch salt

FOR THE SAUCE

4 oz (125g) plain chocolate
½ pint (275ml) very strong black coffee
4 oz (125g) soft brown sugar
2 teaspoons cocoa powder
1 teaspoon vanilla essene
1 oz (25g) butter

fresh strawberries or raspberries and
mint leaves, to decorate

This pudding is one I devised nearly twenty years ago. The moccha sauce can be replaced with either a raspberry or apricot coulis – depending on how you feel and what you have available.

To make the pralines, put the sugar and almonds in a thick-bottomed saucepan; dissolve the sugar then raise the heat to caramelise. Stir with a wooden spoon to coat the almonds with the golden brown mixture. Turn out on to a lightly oiled tin and allow to cool. Then grind to a powder in a food processor.

Whip the cream with the Tia Maria until it holds its shape, fold in the praline powder and then the egg whites, stiffly beaten with a pinch of salt. Pour into lightly oiled individual ramekins and freeze for at least 4 hours.

Melt the chocolate with the coffee, sugar and cocoa. Boil rapidly until beginning to go fudge-like. Remove from the heat and stir in the vanilla and butter. Unmould the frozen soufflés on to individual serving plates and surround each with warm moccha sauce. Garnish the top of the soufflés with a strawberry or a couple of raspberries and a mint leaf.

Irene Canning

GIBSON'S · CARDIFF

Gibson's has been open for eighteen years and specialises in French cuisine. Suppliers include Vin Sullivan of Abergavenny for game, Sadler's of Penarth for fish and meat, Peaches of Cardiff for fruit and vegetables. This is the dinner party menu for the time when you want to see your friends but simply haven't the time to cook an elaborate meal; you need about one hour two days in advance and one hour on the day. The ingredients are easily available and inexpensive enough to afford a lovely gutsy Californian white wine (Parson's Creek would be excellent) or even a Meursault.

SMOKED HADDOCK BAVAROIS

Serves 6

about 10 oz (275g) smoked haddock
milk
mayonnaise
aspic powder
pepper
lemon juice
salad leaves, to serve

Instead of haddock, this can be made with salmon, with a garnish of smoked salmon, or, here in Wales, sewin. It can be made one or two days in advance and served with strips of sesame toast; lightly toast the bread, butter, sprinkle with white sesame seeds and grill.

Poach the fish in milk until it flakes easily with a fork. Drain and discard the skin and bones. From now on, work by volume. Measure the fish with a cup. You will need equal quantities of aspic (liquid) and mayonnaise. Make the aspic up extra strong, using twice as much powder as usual, then cool.

Put the equal quantities of ingredients into a blender or food processor and whirl; taste and season with pepper and lemon juice. Pour into a bowl or moulds and leave to set. Serve with decorative salad leaves.

TURKEY ESCALOPES WITH CUCUMBER AND CHIVES

Serves 6

4 oz (125g) butter
a little oil
1½–2 lbs (700–900g) turkey escalopes
1 large cucumber, peeled, deseeded and cubed
small piece green ginger, finely sliced
scant ½ pint (275ml) dry white wine
scant ½ pint (275ml) well-seasoned chicken stock
1 dessertspoon cornflour
scant dessertspoon grain mustard
bunch of chives, snipped

If funds allow, you can use veal escalopes instead of turkey.

Melt the butter in a large frying pan with a little oil to stop it browning. Seal the turkey on both sides and remove from pan. Add the cucumber and ginger, stir around a little and add the wine and chicken stock. Replace the turkey and simmer for 5 minutes.

Dissolve the cornflour in a little stock or water and add, stirring, to the sauce. Add the mustard and chives to taste.

CHOCOLATE BRANDY CREAM

Serves 6

2 eggs
salt
12 oz (350g) plain chocolate
1 pint (570ml) single cream
4 tablespoons brandy

This can be made two days in advance.

Beat the eggs with a large pinch of salt. Break the chocolate into a blender goblet or food processor. Heat the cream to boiling point, pour on to the chocolate and blend until the chocolate has dissolved.

Add the brandy and beaten eggs, whirl to mix and make sure the bubbles have subsided before pouring into a bowl or individual pots. Serve with a float of brandy or cream and crisp biscuits.

Julia Chalkley

GILBERT'S · LONDON

When my partner, Ann Wregg, and I first opened Gilbert's, we had lino on the floor, plastic tablecloths and paper napkins on the tables. Our aim was to offer good food which tasted of itself in relaxed and welcoming surroundings. Three years later the lino and the plastic have been replaced with carpet and laundered linen, but our precepts for food and service remain unchanged. Each of the following dishes has a distinctive taste – the taste of its principal ingredient. Their sauces depend upon precise seasoning and good base ingredients. The Stilton must be mature but not over ripe, the chicken free range, the tomato sauce simmered long and slow with red wine and vegetables and the chocolate the best bitter variety available.

STILTON AND WALNUT TART

Serves 6 – 8

8 oz (225g) Stilton
2 eggs
2 egg yolks
8 oz (225g) crème fraîche or sour cream
1 x 8 inch (20.5cm) tart shell, uncooked
handful coarsely chopped walnuts

Place the Stilton and eggs in a food processor and process until smooth. Add the cream and process briefly to mix – no seasoning will be necessary. Pour the mixture into the tart case and sprinkle with the chopped walnuts. Bake at 375°F/190°C/Gas 5 for 45 minutes. Cover lightly with foil when nicely browned and serve warm.

HERB BAKED CHICKEN À NOTRE FAÇON

Serves 6

6 free range chicken legs (ask butcher to bone out the legs and divide each into 2 neat pieces, thigh and drumstick)
3 tablespoons fresh breadcrumbs and herbes de Provence mixed in equal quantities

FOR THE SAUCE

4 oz (125g) chicken livers
½ pint (275ml) good homemade tomato sauce
double cream and Madeira (or good full-bodied but dry sherry such as Palo Cortado) to taste
salt and freshly ground black pepper

Season each piece of chicken, roll neatly into shape and place skin side up on a buttered baking sheet. Brush the chicken pieces with melted butter and season again. Sprinkle with the breadcrumb and herb mixture. Roast for 20 minutes at 400°F/200°C/Gas 6.

To make the sauce, sauté the chicken livers gently in a little butter. Blend in a liquidiser with the tomato sauce. Add the cream, Madeira and seasoning to your taste. Blend until quite smooth.

To serve, heat the sauce and pour on to warm plates. Place the chicken on top.

CHOCOLATE TIPSY CAKE

Serves 6 – 8

sponge fingers
rum
½ lb (225g) best quality plain (bitter) chocolate
½ pint (275ml) double cream
1 oz (25g) sifted icing sugar
4 oz (125g) ground almonds
2 tablespoons extra rum

Line a 1 pint (570ml) rectangular metal loaf tin with sponge fingers dipped in rum. Cut the biscuits to fit the height of the tin. Line the sides and base, but not the ends of the tin.

Melt the chocolate gently and cool slightly. Whip the cream softly and fold in the sugar and almonds. Add the chocolate and rum, stirring just enough to mix completely. Pour into the tin and chill until set.

To serve, unmould and cut between the sponge fingers with a hot, wet knife. Serve at room temperature with a chilled homemade vanilla egg custard.

Hilary Chapman

CHEDDINGTON COURT · BEAMINSTER

As a cook I am very interested in the source of the ingredients I use. We only buy fresh fish which mostly comes from Brixham, via Phil Bowditch of Taunton. We also only use free range eggs from a farm in Beaminster, and we are now able to get chickens and meat from The Real Company of Warminster and the Pure Meat Company of Moretonhampstead, Devon. I think it is worth paying a bit extra to know that the animals have been well treated and reared without the use of growth promoters and under free range conditions. (It costs a little more but tastes much better). It is sometimes difficult to be absolutely sure of the source of everything we have to use but it is essential to make an effort to relieve the unnatural treatment and unnecessary suffering of animals and birds where possible.

CHICKEN SALAD WITH CORIANDER AND GINGER DRESSING

Serves 4

FOR THE DRESSING

1 shallot, finely chopped
1 clove garlic, chopped
1 tablespoon soy sauce
6 crushed coriander seeds
4 fl oz (125ml) chicken stock
4 fl oz (125ml) dry white wine
2 tablespoons honey
5 tablespoons sesame oil

FOR THE SALAD

6 oz (175g) cooked chicken breast, shredded
1 small head curly endive
1 small head radicchio
few small spinach leaves
⅛ iceberg lettuce, shredded
few sliced bamboo shoots
3 spring onions, cut fine
3 heads broccoli, blanched and divided into florets

FOR THE GARNISH

1 oz (25g) whole blanched almonds, toasted
coriander leaves, snipped
½ oz (10g) tender root ginger, peeled and cut into fine strips
1 poppadom, cooked and crumbled

Simmer all the ingredients for the dressing, except for the sesame oil, in a small saucepan for 5 minutes. Reduce to 4 fl oz (125ml). Cool, then strain. Whisk in the sesame oil or mix in a liquidiser to emulsify.

Wash and spin dry the salad leaves and carefully mix all the ingredients together. Divide between 4 plates.

Toss each bowl of salad with the dressing or give each person a tiny bowl of dressing, then sprinkle with the ingredients for the garnish.

FILLET OF BRILL IN FILO PASTRY WITH PRAWN BUTTER

Serves 4

FOR THE PRAWN BUTTER

2 oz (50g) unsalted butter
2 oz (50g) chopped prawns
pinch powdered mace
pinch white pepper

FOR THE SAUCE

fish bones
1 pint (570ml) cold water
5 fl oz (150ml) white wine
1 onion, chopped
1 leek, chopped
few white peppercorns
4 fl oz (125ml) double cream
½ oz (10g) kneaded butter
(equal quantities flour and butter)

4 sheets filo pastry, 6 x 8 inches (15 x 20.5cm)
1 lb (450g) fillet of brill, trimmed,
boned and cut into 4
melted butter
egg wash
whole prawns, to garnish

To make the prawn butter, mix together all the ingredients in a food processor, or beat by hand in a bowl. Form into a roll and refrigerate until ready to use.

Simmer all the ingredients for the sauce, except the cream and butter, for 20 minutes. Strain, then return to the pan and reduce to 6 fl oz (175ml). Stir in the double cream, bring to the boil and season. Whisk in the butter and keep the sauce warm in a bain-marie.

Brush each sheet of filo pastry lightly with melted butter and fold in half. Place a piece of fish on each sheet and season. (If the fillets are thin, the pastry can be folded again). Put a knob of prawn butter on each before folding the pastry over the fish, tucking in the ends to make 4 parcels. Keep on oiled paper until ready to use.

Brush each parcel with egg wash or melted butter. Cook the fish, well spaced on a baking tray, near the top of the oven at 375°F/190°C/Gas 5 for about 15 minutes until the pastry is golden brown.

To serve, surround each parcel with a little sauce, whisking any surplus prawn butter into the sauce. Garnish with a few whole prawns and serve with small new potatoes, broccoli and sweetcorn or mange-tout.

COFFEE JELLY WITH AMARETTO

Serves 4

1 pint (570ml) water
about 2 tablespoons sugar
3 level tablespoons powdered coffee
(or 1 pint (570ml) strong brewed coffee)
½ oz (10g) powdered gelatine
4 tablespoons Amaretto (or Tia Maria)
7 fl oz (200ml) double cream
2 teaspoons honey
pinch powdered cinnamon

Bring the water, sugar and coffee to the boil, then reduce the heat. Sprinkle with the gelatine and stir until it has dissolved. Remove from the heat and add the liqueur. Pour into a bowl and place in a larger bowl of iced water to cool.

When the coffee mixture is syrupy, pour about two-thirds of it into tall wine glasses or champagne glasses. Chill until almost set. Whisk the remaining jelly with 5 fl oz (150ml) of the cream until frothy and pour it into the glasses over the jelly. Leave to set; the jellies will not be very stiff. Whisk the remaining cream with the honey and a pinch of cinnamon to taste and put a blob on top of each glass.

Sally Clarke

CLARKE'S · LONDON

Every night of the week we offer a fixed, no-choice menu of 4 courses. I plan the menus to show the best from the market, designed to show a balance between colour, texture and flavour. I prefer light, uncomplicated dishes without the unnecessary addition of butter or cream so that the customer feels satisfied, not over-full, at the end of the meal. Organic salads, herbs and vegetables are bought on a regular basis from suppliers in Kent, Suffolk and the Continent. Fresh fish, including tuna, swordfish, baby squid and cuttlefish, arrives every week from the Boulogne markets. Constant contact with suppliers allows me to keep the menus ever-changing and exciting.

PUMPKIN SOUP

Serves 6

*1 medium pumpkin
(preferably green-skinned variety)
1 cup good olive oil
6 cloves garlic, crushed
1 tablespoon chopped fresh sage
1 large onion, roughly chopped
1 leek, roughly chopped
2 sticks celery, roughly chopped
½ fennel bulb, roughly chopped
2 small red chilli, chopped very fine, with seeds
2 teaspoons salt
vegetable oil and salt, for roasting pumpkin seeds
virgin olive oil and parsley, for garnishing*

Cut the pumpkin into quarters, scoop out the seeds and reserve. Peel the pumpkin with a sharp knife and cut the flesh into roughly 1 inch (2.5 cm) cubes.

Warm the olive oil in a heavy, wide-based pan with the garlic and sage until the aroma is released. Do not allow to burn. Add the vegetables to the pan together with the pumpkin. Stir well over a medium heat until the vegetables begin to soften. Cover with water and bring to the boil, then simmer gently, half-covered, until all the vegetables are soft. Ladle into a food processor and blend until very smooth. Pass the soup through a medium-fine sieve into a clean pan, adjusting consistency and taste by adding water and salt if necessary.

Wash the pumpkin seeds well under a cold running tap to release the strings of flesh. Lay the cleaned seeds on a baking tray, drizzle with a little vegetable oil and sprinkle generously with salt. Bake for 10–15 minutes in a medium to hot oven, turning with a spoon occasionally, until they are golden brown and crisp to the bite.

Serve in warm soup plates sprinkled with the seeds and garnished with parsley and a drizzle of virgin olive oil.

GRILLED CHUMP CHOP OF LAMB WITH ROSEMARY AND GARLIC

Serves 4

4 equally shaped chump chops of lamb
2 cloves fresh garlic, crushed to a paste with salt
3 teaspoons very finely chopped fresh rosemary
4 tablespoons vegetable oil
generous amount freshly ground black pepper

Trim each chop of any excess fat and place on a plate. Mix the garlic, rosemary, oil and pepper well together and smear each chop with the mixture, making sure that each side is well coated. Leave, loosely covered, in a cool place for up to 4 hours to marinate.

Ideally the chops are best charcoal-grilled over a medium-high heat, turning often as they cook, but if this is impossible, the grill or salamander of a conventional oven would be satisfactory. Preheat the grill for 10–15 minutes on the highest setting and cook the chops for 3–4 minutes each side, depending on their thickness and 'doneness' preferred. For medium rare chops, they should feel slightly resistant when gently pressed with the back of a spoon. Remove the chops to a warm plate and cover loosely while the accompanying vegetables are being cooked. This will allow the meat fibres to 'relax' making the meat even more tender.

Serve with a selection of autumn or summer vegetables tossed in herb butter.

NECTARINES FILLED WITH ALMOND

Serves 4

3 oz (75g) unblanched almonds
3 oz (75g) softened unsalted butter
2 oz (50g) caster sugar, plus extra for sprinkling
8 Amaretti biscuits, crushed
4 large ripe nectarines
5 fl oz (150ml) fresh orange juice

Set the oven to 375°F/190°C/Gas 5. Warm the almonds in the oven for 5–10 minutes or until they become slightly crisp. Allow to cool and chop finely.

Beat the butter with the sugar until fluffy, then fold in the crushed biscuits and almonds. Cut each nectarine in half and remove the stone. Place in a baking dish large enough to hold all the nectarines snugly. Pour the orange juice over and sprinkle with a little sugar.

Place an eighth of the almond mixture into each indentation. Bake, uncovered, for 15–20 minutes or until the filling is crisp and the nectarines are tender. Serve warm or chilled with lightly whipped cream.

Veronica Colley

Little Barwick House is a Georgian dower house with an attractive garden on the edge of Barwick park just outside Yeovil in Somerset. We have had our country house restaurant with rooms for eight years now, and as it is our home, people enjoy the relaxed atmosphere we seem to have created. I use fresh seasonal produce, most of which comes from the area; summer vegetables from a neighbour's garden, potatoes from a nearby farmer and fruit from a local grower. Our fish comes from Bridport and our meat from Shepton Mallet. Of course we always have some mature Somerset Cheddar and a local goats cheese; we smoke trout ourselves and make extensive use of the game which is readily available from the area in season.

LITTLE POT OF CURRIED KIDNEYS

Serves 4

6 fresh lamb's kidneys (about 1½ per person)
breadcrumbs
butter, for frying
1 onion, finely chopped
2 teaspoons mild curry paste
½ pint (275ml) double cream

This makes a good supper dish with some crispy French bread and salad. We use a lot of loins of lamb from a local butcher and hence often have fresh kidneys.

Prepare the kidneys in the usual way – cut in half, remove the core and slice each half into small chunks.

Fry the breadcrumbs in butter until just beginning to crisp, then leave to cool.

Sauté the onion in 1 tablespoon butter until softened, add the curry paste and cook gently for another 2 minutes; set aside in a bowl.

Add some more butter to the pan and toss the pieces of kidney in it until sealed. Leave in a sieve to drain (discard this liquid). Mix together the kidneys and onions and put into small 4–5 fl oz (125–150ml) pots. Pour on the cream until the pot is two-thirds full and stir well. Put on to a tray in a hot oven for about 5 minutes until the sauce begins to bubble.

Stir each pot again and put a good layer of breadcrumbs on top. Return to the oven until golden brown and bubbling. The result should be lightly cooked kidney in a creamy curried sauce with a crisp topping!

RED MULLET WITH TOMATO AND SAFFRON SAUCE

Serves 4

2 shallots, chopped
1 clove garlic, crushed
olive oil
2 lbs (900g) tomatoes, skinned and chopped
5 fl oz (150ml) dry white wine
½ sachet saffron powder
thyme
salt and pepper
pinch sugar
4 x red mullet, about 8 oz (225g) each,
scaled and cleaned
flour
chopped parsley

I get my fish from West Bay and the mullet are very fresh. This year they were quite plentiful, though not up to the 5000 seen in Weymouth Bay in August 1891! This information is from Jane Grigson's book on fish in which she gives a similar recipe for cold red mullet.

Fry the shallots and garlic in olive oil until softened. Add the chopped tomatoes and simmer until softened and thickened. Add the wine, saffron, thyme, salt and pepper and cook gently until the sauce thickens, adding a little sugar if the sauce is too tart.

Coat the prepared mullet lightly with flour. Heat about 3–5 tablespoons olive oil in a large frying pan and fry the mullet for 5–7 minutes each side until cooked.

Reheat the sauce and spoon on to one side of each plate with the mullet alongside. Sprinkle the sauce with the parsley.

INDIVIDUAL ALMOND PRALINE BAVAROIS

Serves 6

1½ oz (40g) whole unblanched almonds
1½ oz (40g) granulated sugar
oil
1½ pints (900ml) milk
4 oz (125g) caster sugar
6 egg yolks
few drops almond essence
4 level teaspoons powdered gelatine
7–10 fl oz (200–275ml) double cream

Put the almonds and sugar in a small saucepan; heat gently until the sugar melts and caramelises; do not stir but gently tilt the pan so that the almonds are covered. Tip out on to a lightly oiled baking sheet and leave to harden. When cold, break up roughly, place in a blender or food processor and grind to a fairly fine powder; reserve 6 almonds for decoration.

Gently heat the milk with 2 oz (50g) of the caster sugar until the sugar has dissolved. Cream the egg yolks with the remaining sugar until thick and light, then pour on to the hot milk, stirring continuously. Return to the saucepan and stir over a very low heat until the mixture coats the back of a spoon. Do not boil or the custard will curdle. Strain the mixture, add almond essence and whisk thoroughly.

Sprinkle the gelatine with 4 tablespoons water, leave to soak for 5 minutes, then heat gently to dissolve. Stir quickly into the custard and refrigerate for 15–20 minutes or until the custard begins to thicken.

Lightly whip the cream until it just begins to hold its shape and is about the same consistency as the custard. Fold 3 tablespoons of the cream into the custard and pour or spoon into 6 lightly oiled straight-sided ramekins. Refrigerate for at least 4 hours until set.

Turn out the Bavarois on to serving plates and cover each one with a thick layer of the remaining (just firm) cream. Sprinkle the praline to cover all surfaces and decorate with a whole caramelised almond.

Mellanie Dixon

CIBOURE · LONDON

There were two important factors which brought me into 'food' and they stem from my rural upbringing on a farm.
Firstly there was the thrill of growing a wonderful selection of fruit and vegetables followed by the luxury of cooking and eating them only minutes after harvest; the flavour was, and still is, out of this world.
Secondly we reared beef cattle and an assortment of exotic poultry and game. It was very satisfying to watch all these creatures grow and respond to your care which was quite demanding, especially when it involved twenty-four hour nursing and the odd rescue in a blizzard. But sadly the day of execution inevitably came. After all the time and effort spent by the animals and ourselves, I felt that I owed it to them to make something marvellous and worthwhile out of these wonderful ingredients.

SALAD OF SMOKED GOOSE BREAST WITH WILD MUSHROOMS AND GARLIC

Serves 4

FOR THE DRESSING

½ punnet raspberries, hulled
2 tablespoons raspberry vinegar
1 teaspoon Dijon mustard
2 teaspoons caster sugar
½ pint (275ml) vegetable oil
1 tablespoon olive oil
seasoning

FOR THE SALAD

1 head frisé lettuce with large, yellow-green heart
1 large clove garlic
3 shallots
8 oz (225g) mixed wild mushrooms
1 teaspoon chopped parsley
1 smoked goose breast (or smoked duck or pigeon)

To make the dressing, place the raspberries, vinegar, mustard and sugar in a bowl and beat together with a balloon whisk until smooth. Slowly add the olive oil and vegetable oil, whisking continuously.

Thoroughly wash the frisé lettuce, keeping only the yellowy-green heart, and tear into small pieces. Place a circle of lettuce leaves round the edge of four plates, leaving the centre clear. Sprinkle with the dressing.

Finely chop the garlic and shallots. Rinse and dry the mushrooms, breaking the large ones in two. Sweat the garlic and shallots in a little oil in a frying pan, then add the mushrooms and seasoning. Cook until the mushrooms are soft, then add the parsley. Divide the mixture into four and place in the centre of each plate.

Trim off all but a thin layer of fat from the goose breast and slice thinly. Place the slices in a circle on the lettuce around the edge of the plates. Serve immediately.

GRILLED TUNA WITH ROAST RED PEPPERS AND CORIANDER SAUCE

Serves 4

FOR THE SAUCE

2 bunches fresh coriander
3 large cloves garlic
2 oz (50g) pine nuts
2 tablespoons olive oil
1 tablespoon sesame oil
5 fl oz (150ml) Chinese Shaosing wine
1 tablespoon soya sauce
1 tablespoon Teriyaki marinade
3 teaspoons caster sugar
5 fl oz (150ml) vegetable oil

olive oil
2 red peppers
seasoning
4 tuna steaks

Coriander, sesame oil, Teryaki marinade and Shaosing wine can be bought in any good Chinese supermarket.

Roughly chop the coriander leaves and garlic. Place in a food processor with the pine nuts and reduce to a paste. Slowly add the olive oil, sesame oil, Shaosing wine, soya sauce, Teriyaki marinade, caster sugar and vegetable oil. This sauce will keep for several days in the refrigerator.

Preheat the oven to 400°F/200°C/Gas 6. Place the peppers on a baking sheet with a little olive oil and cook in the hot oven, turning regularly to prevent burning. When soft, allow to cool, then remove skin, core and seeds. Cut into very thin strips and set aside.

Remove any scales and blood from the fish and season both sides. Dip in oil, place on a baking sheet and grill for a couple of minutes each side; the fish should be rare.

Serve the fish in the centre of the plate on top of the coriander sauce and garnish with a lattice of red pepper strips. Serve with a green salad.

CHILLED PASSION FRUIT SOUFFLÉ

Serves 4

8 fl oz (225ml) passion fruit juice
2½ leaves gelatine, soaked in cold water until soft
2 egg yolks
3 oz (75g) caster sugar
8 fl oz (225ml) double cream
4 egg whites
pinch cream of tartar
whipped cream or icing sugar to decorate

Some supermarkets may sell passion fruit juice but if not, scoop out the contents of 16 passion fruit and place in a liquidiser for a count of 30. Pass through a fine sieve and make up to 8 fl oz (225ml) with fresh orange juice.

Heat the passion fruit juice in a stainless steel or heatproof glass bowl over hot water; add the gelatine and dissolve.

Put the egg yolks and 1 oz (25g) of the caster sugar in a bowl over hot water; whisk until the ribbon stage, then add the passion fruit mixture. Refrigerate until it starts to set.

Whip the double cream until thick and fold it into the setting mixture. Whisk the egg whites and cream of tartar to stiff peaks, add the remaining caster sugar, then fold into the passion fruit mixture.

Take four small ramekins, circle with paper to a depth of 4½ inches (11cm) and secure with string or staples. Pour the mixture into the ramekins until it reaches 1½ inches (3.5cm) above the rim of the dish; allow to set.

Run a warm knife around the inside of the paper to release the soufflé and peel off. Decorate with whipped cream or dust with icing sugar.

Gillian Enthoven

LE MESURIER · LONDON

I am very fortunate in the position of my restaurant. On the opposite side of the main road (Old Street, EC1) is the delightful Whitecross Street Market. The street is very Dickensian – long and narrow with small Victorian shops on either side. One of these is a wonderful bakery where we buy all our bread. It has mouthwatering smells of hot crusty bread, juicy doughnuts and every kind of homemade cake. The market is made up of stalls of every size and colour selling everything imaginable. If we run out of anything we simply run across the road and buy anything from asparagus and raspberries to balls of string and bunches of flowers!

CAMEMBERT EN CROÛTE

Serves 6

4 oz (125g) plain flour
pinch salt
4 oz (125g) butter
4 oz (125g) cream or curd cheese
1 x 9 oz (250g) Camembert cheese
(or 1 box portioned Camembert)
few sultanas (optional)
1 egg yolk

Sift the flour and salt together and rub in the butter to a large crumb texture. Blend in the cream cheese with a fork, using your hands when the mixture becomes less sticky. Alternatively mix everything in a food processor, but be careful not to get the flour and butter mixture too sticky or the cream cheese won't blend in. The pastry needs to be well chilled before rolling out.

Heat the oven to 425°F/220°C/Gas 7–8. Roll out the pastry to ¼ inch (0.5cm) thickness. Cut out a circle 9 inches (23cm) in diameter and position the cheese in the centre. Scatter a few sultanas over the top of the cheese, if using. Bring the pastry up and over the cheese, overlapping the upper edge of the cheese by 1 inch (2.5cm). The pastry splits easily so be prepared to patch it if necessary. With the remaining pastry make a disc to fit over the top of the Camembert, pressing it down so that the edges are well sealed. Use scraps of pastry to make flowers and leaves and decorate the surface with them. Mix the egg yolk with 2 teaspoons of cold water and brush it all over the pastry as if laquering a box. The assembled Camembert en Croûte may be left for up to 8 hours in the refrigerator before cooking. Bake for 25 minutes at 425°F/220°C/Gas 7. Allow to cool for a few minutes before serving. Cut the cheese into wedges like a cake – be careful as the liquid cheese will flow out.

As an alternative you can cover individual portions of Camembert with the pastry and serve one or two to your guests, depending on how greedy they are! They are especially delicious served with deep-fried parsley.

MONKFISH IN PERNOD SAUCE

Serves 4

2 oz (50g) butter
2 shallots, chopped
8 tablespooons Pernod
½ pint (275ml) fish stock
8 tablespoons dry white wine
8 fl oz (225ml) double cream
pinch cayenne
salt and pepper
24 oz (550g) net weight monkfish,
filleted and skinned

Melt the butter and fry the shallots until soft. Stir in the Pernod and bring to the boil. Add the fish stock and wine and boil rapidly until reduced by half. Add the cream and continue boiling until reduced and thickened slightly. Season well.

Poach the monkfish fillets very gently in this sauce – they become a beautiful yellow colour as the sauce thickens.

In the restaurant we serve this dish with little balls of different coloured vegetables. Catering shops sell small ball scoops for this purpose. Carrots and courgettes look particularly pretty. The balls are scooped out of the vegetables, blanched for a few minutes, then scattered over the sauce.

HOT LEMON SOUFFLÉ

Serves 4

2 oz (50g) butter, plus extra for buttering dishes
4 oz (125g) sugar, plus extra for sprinkling in dishes
6 tablespoons lemon juice
4 egg yolks
grated zest of 2 lemons
5 egg whites
icing sugar, for dusting

Do not be anxious about cooking soufflés at home; they are easy to prepare ahead and the only last-minute preparation is the whisking of the egg whites – and calm nerves! We have a soufflé, either savoury or sweet, most days at the restaurant and customers are always delighted when their individual soufflé arrives, all puffed and golden.

Butter 4 individual soufflé dishes and sprinkle well with sugar, discarding any excess. In a heavy-based pan (not aluminium) heat the butter with half the sugar and the lemon juice until the butter and sugar have melted. Take off the heat, beat in the egg yolks one by one and add the lemon zest. Heat very gently, whisking constantly until the mixture thickens to the consistency of double cream. Cook the mixture until quite thick but do not allow to get too hot or it will curdle. The soufflé may be prepared 3–4 hours ahead up to this point; keep the mixture covered.

Set the oven to 425°F/220°C/Gas 7 20–30 minutes before serving. Whip the egg whites until very stiff, add the remaining sugar and beat for 20 seconds longer or until glossy. Heat the lemon mixture gently until hot to the touch and stir in about a quarter of the egg white mixture. Fold in the remaining egg whites as lightly as possible.

Spoon into the prepared dishes and bake for about 9–10 minutes or until the soufflé is puffed and brown. Sprinkle it with icing sugar and serve at once. Don't worry if this soufflé doesn't rise amazingly – it will still be light and delicious inside! It also behaves very well if it has to wait a few minutes before serving – just turn the oven off and keep the door shut.

Gunn Eriksen

ALTNAHARRIE INN · ULLAPOOL

Altnaharrie lies on the southern shores of Loch Broom on the north-west coast of Scotland, just opposite the fishing village of Ullapool. The house was originally built a few hundred years ago as a stop-over point for drovers on their way to sell cattle in the south. There is no road by which to reach us but we run a launch at least five times daily – the boat journey takes ten minutes. We have no neighbours, the waves lap at the edge of the garden, and the heather-clad hills offer magnificent walks and the chance of spotting a variety of wild life, including Golden Eagles, seals and otters. Because of our situation we have no mains electricity supply, but we do have our own generator which runs for most of the time – it is switched off when everyone has gone to bed (hence the torch and candle by the bedside!) Every night I cook a five-course dinner for a single sitting, using a wealth of ingredients from the sea and surrounding countryside. Use your own instincts and tastes to guide you when it comes to quantities for the sauces in these recipes.

MEDALLIONS OF SIKA DEER WITH WILD MUSHROOMS AND CHERRIES WITH A SAUCE OF ITS OWN JUICES, JUNIPER AND DILL

2 medallions of sika, approx. 1 inch (2.5cm) thick, per person

FOR THE SAUCE
1 leek, chopped
butter
a few juniper berries
a little red wine
Armagnac
selection of fungi e.g. chanterelles, ceps, birchboletus and oyster mushrooms
a few cherries, quartered
sprigs of dill

Roast the bones from the sika with the leek and a little butter. When browned, put into a pan with the juniper berries, cover with water and simmer for a few hours. Strain into a smaller pan, add a little red wine and reduce. Strain again and again. You should be left with approx. 2 tablespoons per person.

Heat a heavy frying pan, add a knob of butter and fry the medallions for a few seconds on either side. Flambé with a little Armagnac. Remove the meat from the pan and add the juices to the sauce. Taste and adjust for seasoning.

Meanwhile fry in butter a selection of fungi, such as chanterelles, ceps, birchboletus and oyster mushrooms. Put the medallions on plates with a little sauce and arrange the mushrooms and quartered cherries around. Decorate each medallion with a sprig of dill.

SELECTION OF FISH WITH A LITTLE CAKE OF SQUAT LOBSTER AND LEEKS, WITH A SAUCE OF FISH JUICES AND CHAMPAGNE, INLAID WITH A SAUCE OF BITTERCRESS AND CHAMPAGNE

FOR THE CAKE

strudel pastry, small handful sliced leeks per cake
butter, soured cream, pepper, few drops of garlic
juice, chopped dill
4–5 squat lobster (spinies) per person

FOR THE BITTERCRESS SAUCE

½ onion, 1 oz (25g) butter, 5 fl oz (150ml) milk
good handful bittercress leaves, a little champagne
dash cream, salt and pepper

FOR THE FISH JUICE AND CHAMPAGNE SAUCE

reduced fish stock, a little champagne, diced butter
salt and pepper, dash cream

selection of 3–4 different types of fish (see below),
fish stock, white wine, pepper and sea salt

You can use almost any white fish plus salmon or trout. If you are using, say 3–4 different types of fish (e.g. halibut, monk, salmon, witch) you need about 1½–2 inch square of each type per person, and one fillet of witch rolled up. Save all skin and bones for stock.

To make the cake, start by making the strudel pastry. Wash the leeks and soften them gently in butter. Make a mixture of soured cream, pepper, a few drops of garlic juice, the chopped dill and add 4–5 spinies per person. Having pulled the strudel and folded it over (with butter in the middle), cut 8 inch (20cm) squares, put a small handful of leeks in the middle with the shellfish mixture on top, then gently pick up the corners and tie with a thin 'string' of leek. Put into a buttered ovenproof dish and brush with butter. Cook until golden and crisp.

To make the bittercress sauce, sauté the onion in butter until just soft. Add the milk and simmer for a few minutes. Liquidise with the washed bittercress. Put through a sieve, return to the pan and add the champagne, cream and maybe salt and pepper.

For the second sauce, put the reduced fish stock and a little champagne into a small saucepan. Reduce by half. Whisk in a few pieces of butter, little by little, add seasoning, a touch of cream and more champagne if needed. Set sauces aside and keep warm.

Prepare the fish fillet and cut into suitable pieces according to how many species you are using. Put into different ovenproof dishes according to thickness – turbot, for instance, takes longer to cook than, say, witch. Put a little water and wine into the dishes and sprinkle with pepper and sea salt. The cooking varies from oven to oven – don't overcook!

Meanwhile the squat cake should be cooking. Arrange the cake in the middle of the plate, with the fish arranged round. Carefully spoon the fish sauce on to the plate, taking care not to cover the cake nor the fish, then add a little of the bittercress sauce. Decorate with a little bittercress and maybe a whole spiny?

PEAR FLAN WITH CRÈME DE CASSIS

FOR THE PASTRY

4 oz (125g) flour, 3½ oz (100g) butter
2 tablespoons sugar, 1 egg yolk
1 teaspoon lemon juice

4–5 pears, 5 fl oz (150ml) cream, 2 oz (50g) sugar
2 tablespoons crème de cassis

Make the pastry in the usual way and use it to line an 8 inch (20.5cm) flan tin. Bake blind for about 10 minutes at about 425°F/220°C/Gas 7. Halve the pears. Put them into the flan case in the shape of a flower head. Mix the cream, sugar and crème de cassis and pour over the pears. Bake in a moderately hot oven for about 10–15 minutes until the pears are softish. Serve hot with cream, decorate with blackcurrants and pour a little Crème de Cassis around.

Carole Evans

Ever since a small child I have always enjoyed good food, thanks to my mother. My parents always grew vegetables in the garden, my mother bottled and canned fruits, made pickles and jams and as a family we all took part, growing up with an appreciation of good food. Getting married at nineteen years old to a farmer, suddenly I found myself having to cope with all sorts of goodies at the kitchen door. I bought Cordon Bleu magazine for 4/6d a week; unknowingly the commencement of my catering career. I now have a large library used mainly for reference. I would like to think I have found my own style of cooking, using as much local produce as I can, keeping closely to seasons. Customers will phone offering surplus garden produce; one lady brings lavender and honey from our own bees makes wonderful Lavender and Honey ice cream. My greatest pleasure at the conclusion of an evening is that customers leaving the restaurant have had an 'eloquent sufficiency'.

QUAIL EGGS IN FILO PASTRY WITH LEMON HOLLANDAISE SAUCE

Serves 4

FOR THE MUSHROOM DUXELLE
2 shallots or 1 small onion, very finely chopped
1 oz (25g) butter
8 oz (225g) mushrooms
double cream, to finish
salt and pepper

FOR THE LEMON HOLLANDAISE
4 egg yolks
1 tablespoon water
2 tablespoons lemon juice
6 oz (175g) unsalted butter

cayenne pepper
salt and white pepper

2 sheets filo pastry
melted butter
3 quail eggs per person
parsley, to garnish

Soften the shallots in butter until transparent; do not allow to brown. Meanwhile whizz the mushrooms in a processor for a few seconds until they are finely chopped but not puréed. Add to the shallots and continue cooking until the mixture starts to dry on the bottom of the pan when you draw a spoon across. Add the cream and return to the heat; season to taste. The mixture should be a dropping consistency; if it is too wet, cook a little longer. Put on one side to cool. This will keep for 2–3 days in the refrigerator.

To make the Hollandaise, place the egg yolks, water and lemon juice in a food processor and whizz until light and frothy. Melt the butter in a small pan or in the microwave until just melted and pour into the processor through a funnel while the machine is running. Continue to whizz for a few seconds and season to taste. Pour the mixture into a glass bowl and whisk over hot water until light and fluffy – or put the bowl in the microwave, whisking every few seconds until you reach the same stage. Don't panic if the mixture curdles – let it cool slightly, then add a little cold water and continue to whizz. Keep warm over a pan of hot water until needed. This sauce can also be stored in the refrigerator for a few days, straight from the food processor; cook when required.

Cut each sheet of filo pastry into 2 and brush each sheet liberally with melted butter, placing one sheet over the other to form 4 layers. Cut into 4 squares and place over the outside of small brioche moulds or ramekins, trimming off any overhang. Bake at 425°F/220°C/Gas 7 until golden brown. Allow to cool, then remove the cases on to a cooling rack. Keep in an air-tight container until required – they can be made up to 1 week in advance if stored in this way.

Cook the quail eggs in slightly salted boiling water for 2 minutes from boiling, plunging into cold water immediately to prevent over-cooking; they need to be soft in the middle. Crack well all over with a small teaspoon and lift off the shell, breaking and removing the inside skin which is tougher than a hen's egg. Place the shelled eggs in warm water until needed.

Place a small amount of the warmed duxelle in the centre of warmed plates and fix the pastry cases in position. Fill the cases nearly to the top with the duxelle, place 3 eggs in the centre and coat with Hollandaise, allowing a small amount to run down on to the plate. Finish with a sprig of parsley.

PORK TENDERLOIN WRAPPED IN PARMA HAM WITH A MUSTARD SAUCE

Serves 4

2 pork tenderloins, trimmed, about 1lb 12 oz (825g)
6–8 prunes, stoned and cut in half lengthways
4 slices Parma ham
small amount of caul (you may need to order this in advance from your butcher)

FOR THE MUSTARD SAUCE

½ pint (275ml) strong chicken stock reduced to 5 fl oz (150ml)
1 tablespoon Pommery mustard
4 fl oz (125ml) double cream
dash brandy
salt and pepper
watercress or parsley, to garnish

Make an incision with a small sharp knife along the full length of the tenderloin. Roll up the meat and push the prunes through the centre of the tenderloin.

Coat the base of a small frying pan sparingly with oil and heat until smoking. Seal the meat on all sides, remove from the pan and allow to cool. When cool, roll the tenderloin up neatly in the slices of Parma ham.

Have the caul in warm water ready to use. Take a small amount and spread out on a work surface – you will be surprised how far it will stretch. Place the tenderloin wrapped in ham on to the caul and cover it completely; this is not only to secure the ham but to baste the tenderloin while cooking. Cook for 20 minutes at 425°F/220°C/Gas 7 and let it stand for a further 10 minutes.

To make the mustard sauce, add the mustard to the chicken stock in a small pan, bring to the boil and simmer for a few minutes. Add the cream, bring back to the boil and reduce until a good creamy consistency, adding a touch of brandy if you are feeling generous. Season to taste.

When ready to serve, carve each tenderloin into two and arrange on top of the sauce on warmed plates. Garnish with a sprig of watercress or parsley.

APPLE SOUFFLÉ

Serves 4

4 large apples (Golden Delicious or Coxes)
1 teaspoon unsalted butter, melted
lemon juice

FOR THE SOUFFLÉ

2 egg yolks
4 egg whites
2 oz (50g) caster sugar
lemon juice
1 tablespoon King Offa cider brandy (or Calvados)
icing sugar

FOR THE APPLE GARNISH

3 apple slices per person
butter
lemon juice
icing sugar

vanilla ice cream and double cream, to serve

Cut the tops off the apples just above the fattest part. Make a cross in the flesh and with a spoon scoop out the centre of the apple, leaving a wall about ¼ inch (0.5cm) thick. Mix together the melted butter and lemon juice and brush the insides of the apples to prevent them turning brown. Cover with clingfilm and store in the refrigerator until needed – this can be done earlier in the day.

In a medium-sized mixing bowl cream together the egg yolks and 1 oz (25g) of the caster sugar until light and fluffy. In a second bowl whisk the egg whites with the remaining sugar until you have soft peaks. Add a squeeze of lemon juice and whip until very firm.

Add the brandy and a little of the whisked egg whites to the egg yolks and stir well. Gently fold in the rest of the egg white and fill the apples with the mixture. Dust the tops with icing sugar and bake in a medium oven (375°F/190°C/Gas 5) for 12 minutes.

Butter a baking sheet well and place the apple slices on it. Spread them with butter, squeeze lemon juice over and dredge well with icing sugar. Place under a hot grill to caramelize. This can be done while the soufflés are cooking.

Arrange the apple slices on one side of each plate and serve with vanilla ice cream and double cream as soon as the soufflés come out of the oven. I like to put a rosebud or flower on the plate for colour. This is a complicated dish, but once mastered will impress all your friends!

Ann Fitzgerald

THE FARMHOUSE KITCHEN · MATHRY

We have been open now for six years. Our aim is to present dishes that people just do not have time these days to do for themselves. A dish will not be added to the repertoire unless it comes from an established tradition and has some style and excitement about it. Sauces are all-important as is the use of the best materials available.

We do not cater for calorie watchers; we expect people to be hungry when they come here and to have a liking for dairy products, wine, brandy, game, meat and fish. We do not cook lamb, beef and fish to the point of lifelessness unless ordered to do so. Even then my heart sinks when I am told to cook a well-done tournedo as I know it is impossible to impress anyone with vulcanised meat whatever the accompanying sauce. Similarly with fish; we have the best, freshest materials that it is possible for anyone to lay their hands on but if this wonderful sewin, turbot, brill, sole or halibut is to be cooked past the point of juiciness, then the fish might just as well have come down from Grimsby.

We have found it possible over the years to build up an efficient network of supply. Within 24 hours of ordering, this restaurant in remote Pembrokeshire can be supplied with Gressingham duck, guinea fowl, grouse and wild venison in prime condition from Cumbria; tiger prawns, eels, rascasse, clams, hare and soft-shelled crab from Abergavenny. Within 36 hours we can get Bresse squabs from the South of France, again in beautiful condition. Lobsters, crabs, langouste and scallops, mussels, oysters and white fish come in all the time from local suppliers.

SCALLOPS BAKED IN FILO PASTRY WITH LEMON BEURRE BLANC

Serves 4

FOR EACH PERSON

1 sheet filo pastry
melted butter
2 dressed scallops
1 teaspoon double cream
pinch chopped oregano
1 tablespoon Armagnac or Cognac

FOR THE BEURRE BLANC

½ pint (275ml) hock or other medium white wine
1 shallot, finely chopped
lemon juice
diced, chilled butter
1 red or green pepper, diced

Filo pastry comes in a pack which can be kept frozen, or in the refrigerator for a couple of days. It is not really difficult to handle but will not take to being exposed to the air for long, so work speedily.

Cut a rectangle of filo pastry about 12 x 6 inches (30.5 x 15cm) and brush one side of it with melted butter. Fold it in half to make a 6 inch (15cm) square and butter the uppermost side. Place a scallop in the centre of the pastry square, top with a dollop of cream, a little chopped oregano, a tablespoon of Armagnac or Cognac and seasoning.

Draw up each corner of the filo square to meet at the top, and squeeze together to seal, turning down each tip to give a floral effect. Butter the outside of the filo purse and bake for 8–10 minutes in the hottest oven you have. Cooking times may vary – the scallop will be cooked when the tips of the pastry begin to blacken.

Make the sauce while the scallops are cooking. Put the white wine in a saucepan with the chopped shallot and lemon juice and cook briskly for a few minutes until the wine is reduced by half. Then whisk in a few squares of butter straight from the fridge, ensuring that you whisk thoroughly, leaving no oily remains. Keep the sauce warm.

Scatter the diced pepper around the edge of the plate and place the cooked scallop in the centre. Strain the beurre blanc around the filo purse over the diced pepper.

ROAST LAMB PROVENÇAL

Serves 2

1 best end of lamb
breadcrumbs
chopped aniseed, parsley or chervil
dried Provençal herbs
olive oil
1 clove garlic, chopped

FOR THE SAUCE

1 onion, chopped
1 lb (450g) tomatoes, chopped
few mushrooms, chopped
1 stick celery, chopped
½ pint (275ml) dry white wine
salt and pepper
chopped fresh rosemary and basil

Ask your butcher for a best end of lamb, chine bone removed, with seven or eight chops. Trim the lamb by inserting a sharp knife under the thickish layer of skin and fat and easing it off. This will expose the eye or fillet and pieces of coarse meat attached to the bones. Take off these pieces and put into a pan with ½ pint (275ml) boiling water. Saw off the ends of the chop bones, leaving about 2 inches (5cm) attached to the fillet, and put the bones in the stock pot as well.

Mix the breadcrumbs with the chopped and dried herbs and garlic. Paint the outside of the lamb with olive oil and press the crumb and herb mixture on to it so that it is evenly coated. Keep the lamb in the fridge while you prepare the sauce.

Sauté the chopped vegetables in a covered pan, stirring from time to time. After about 15 minutes, when plenty of tomato juice has been released, force the vegetables through a chinois or conical sieve. Really squeeze the vegetables and extract all the juice, then add the white wine and stock. Cook until you reach the desired consistency, then add seasoning and the rosemary and basil. Keep the sauce warm.

Cook the lamb for 20–25 minutes in the top of a very hot oven on a wire rack placed over a tin to catch the juices and add to the sauce. Allow to rest in a cooler oven 300°F/150°C/Gas 2 for about 10 minutes.

To serve, pour a pool of the sauce into the middle of a hot plate. Cut the lamb into chops and place on top of the sauce.

CHOCOLATE MILLE-FEUILLES

Serves 4

9 oz (250g) plain chocolate (Cadbury's is ideal)
1 whole egg, plus 1 yolk
7 fl oz (200ml) double cream (Jersey is ideal)
rum

This is a way we have devised of serving a rum-laden chocolate mousse. The secret in getting the mousse to set, with its generous proportion of liqueur, is the use of the extra egg yolk rather than a whole egg. It always sets no matter how much rum goes in.

To make the mousse, melt 5 oz (150g) of the chocolate over a pan of boiling water. Watch it carefully, stirring so that it does not become gritty. Beat the eggs and egg yolks thoroughly in a mixer. They are ready only when the foam falls slowly off the whisk when it is pulled out of the mixture. They cannot be beaten too much.

Add a teaspoon of cold water to the cream and beat to a 'peak' consistency.

Beat the chocolate slowly, but in one go, into the beaten eggs, then slowly add the cream, this time in 2 parts, to the mixture. The mixture should be silky with no little lumps of cream. Now add the rum – this is a matter of taste but I have found that it will take up to a quarter of a bottle.

Pour the mixture into a bowl and leave in the ice compartment of the fridge to set for 4–6 hours.

While the mousse is setting, make some chocolate sheets. Melt the remainder of the chocolate as before. Spread a sheet of baking parchment on a flat surface. When the chocolate has reached a semi-runny consistency, paint it on to the parchment with a kitchen brush in long sheets about 1½ inches (3.5 cm) wide. Mark the sheets lightly with a knife into 4 inch (10 cm) lengths and leave to set – this will take an hour or so in winter. When the sheets are firm with a matt finish, run a thin blade under them to separate them from the parchment and keep them in a cool place.

To assemble, place a sheet of chocolate on a cold plate, cover it with a thin layer of mousse, another sheet of chocolate, another layer of mousse topped with a third sheet of chocolate. Any left-over mousse should be kept at the temperature at which it was set.

Josie Fawcett

THE CROMWELLIAN · KIRKHAM

When we first took over The Cromwellian Restaurant four years ago, we maintained its standing as a French restaurant. This fitted in with my formal training at Leicester Domestic Science College where I specialised in French Cuisine in my final year, together with subsequent experiences in France. As time went by, we found ourselves being asked the question, Why in a restaurant called the Cromwellian occupying a historic seventeenth century building, in a Lancashire town of its own long heritage, were we serving French food? So we gradually introduced British dishes starting with black pudding and later followed by the introduction of hot British puddings. These were often traditional dishes such as Rhubarb Brown Betty and Queen of Puddings or sometimes our own derivation such as Chocolate Orange Sponge with Hot Chocolate Sauce. Our restaurant offers a fixed price three course menu with four or five choices at each of these courses. Such has been the popularity of our change in direction that our metamorphosis is complete and we are now a thoroughly British restaurant in a thoroughly British Lancashire town.

FILO PASTRY WITH CHICKEN AND BOURSIN

Serves 4

8 oz (225g) cooked diced chicken
4 oz (125g) boursin cheese
1 small egg
seasoning
2 sheets filo pastry, 8 ins x 12 ins (20.5 x 30.5cm)
melted butter

FOR THE SAUCE
2½ fl oz (60ml) dry white wine
2½ fl oz (60ml) double cream
1 teaspoon chopped fresh herbs
sprigs of fresh herbs to garnish

Mix the chicken, cheese and beaten egg together and season. Separate the sheets of filo pastry and brush the first with melted butter. Place the other sheet on top and brush with melted butter. Divide into 8 equal sized pieces. Spoon the mixture into the centre of each piece of pastry and gather the tops together like a money purse. Place on a greased baking tray and bake in a pre-heated oven at 425°F/220°C/ Gas 7 for 7–8 minutes until golden brown and crisp.

To make the sauce, heat together the wine and cream until you have the desired consistency and add the chopped herbs. Serve two parcels per portion on a warm plate, surrounded by the sauce and garnished with a sprig of fresh herbs.

RONDELLE OF SOLE WITH SMOKED SALMON AND LEMON BUTTER

Serves 4

8 oz (225g) smoked salmon
2 small lemon sole, skinned and filleted
seasoning
1 teaspoon fresh dill

FOR THE LEMON BUTTER

juice of half a lemon
2 teaspoons finely chopped shallots
4 fl oz (125ml) fish stock
1 oz (25g) unsalted butter
4 fl oz (125ml) double cream
lemon zest, for garnishing

Lightly grease a sheet of foil and place the flattened smoked salmon on it to make an 8 inch (20.5cm) square. Place the flattened sole on top and season with salt, pepper and herbs. Carefully roll up as tightly as possible, like a Swiss roll, enclosing in tin foil. Make sure it is well sealed, especially at the ends, and steam for about 10–15 minutes. Allow to stand for a few minutes before slicing carefully.

To make the sauce, place the lemon juice, shallots and fish stock in a pan and reduce until a light, creamy consistency. Stir in the butter and cream, season and reheat.

Serve the Rondelles of Sole on a warm plate on a circle of the sauce and garnish with blanched julienne of lemon zest.

BANANA, BUTTERSCOTCH AND WALNUT WHOLEFOOD CRUMBLE

Serves 4

FOR THE TOPPING

3 oz (75g) butter
2 oz (50g) wholemeal flour
2 oz (50g) plain flour
2 oz (50g) rolled oats
3 oz (75g) demerara sugar

FOR THE BUTTERSCOTCH SAUCE

2 oz (50g) butter
3 oz (75g) soft brown sugar
2 oz (50g) granulated sugar
12 oz (350g) golden syrup
2½ fl oz (60ml) double cream
drop vanilla essence

4 bananas
2 oz (50g) walnuts

To make the butterscotch sauce, put the butter, sugar and syrup into a heavy pan over a low heat. When liquid, stir and cook for about 10 minutes. Allow to cool slightly and stir in the cream and vanilla essence. (The sauce may be kept for up to a month in a screw top jar in the fridge).

To make the topping, rub the butter into the flour and oats, then stir in the sugar. Slice the bananas, mix with the walnuts and place in the bottom of an ovenproof dish. Pour over enough butterscotch sauce to sweeten and sprinkle the crumble mixture on top.

Place in a pre-heated oven at 400°F/200°C/Gas 6 for about 20 minutes. Serve hot or cold with fresh cream.

Toni Ferguson-Lees

LANDGATE BISTRO · RYE

Living in Rye, which has its own fishing fleet, we get the very freshest fish and shellfish in season. Romney Marsh provides an abundance of game, wild duck, hares, rabbits and pigeons. Our excellent local butcher provides us with the justly prized Romney Marsh lamb, wonderful especially when milk-fed in the late spring. We have a local supplier who grows a variety of unusual salad leaves and herbs organically as well as raising guinea fowl and quail for us. We try to have a large variety of seasonal vegetables to choose from, including kohlrabi, pink fir apple potatoes and purées, swedes, carrots, parsnips and sprouts. The basis of most of our dishes is a really well-flavoured stock made from the bones of the appropriate fish or bird, with the minimum of cooking for fish and breast meat especially and no frilly presentation!

SQUID BRAISED WITH WHITE WINE, TOMATOES AND GARLIC

Serves 6

2½–3 lbs (1.15–1.4kg) squid
(larger ones are better for this long cooking)
2 tablespoons olive oil
4 cloves garlic, crushed
½ teaspoon salt
1 teaspoon pepper
1 lb (450g) tomatoes (as red as possible) chopped
5 fl oz (150ml) dry white wine
2 tablespoons chopped parsley

Clean the squid, chop the tentacles and cut the body into rings. Heat the oil in a heavy casserole and cook the squid, stirring occasionally, for 10 minutes.

Add the remaining ingredients, except the parsley. Stir well, cover and stew gently for about 1 hour until the squid is very tender, stirring occasionally to prevent sticking. Stir in the parsley and serve.

WILD RABBIT WITH ROSEMARY AND WHITE WINE

Serves 6

*3 very fresh small wild rabbits,
preferably with liver and kidneys
2 tablespoons olive oil
1 oz (25g) butter
1 large onion, thinly sliced
2 cloves garlic, crushed
2 very ripe tomatoes, chopped
1 tablespoon chopped fresh rosemary
½ pint (275ml) dry white wine
water*

For this dish I like to use tender, small wild rabbits, allowing half per person. Rabbit bones are the only kind I do not use for stock as I find the flavour unpleasantly strong.

Remove the livers and kidneys and set aside. Cut off the back legs at the base of the spine (a chopper is useful) and cut through the skin, separating the front legs from the body. Pull off any fat and skin around the legs and rinse. With a sharp knife remove the fillets from either side of the saddle. Cut off the whitish membrane on the outside which would shrink during cooking. Discard the carcass. Dry the legs on kitchen paper.

Melt the butter and oil in a heavy casserole and add the rabbit legs with the onion and garlic. Cook over a medium heat for 5 minutes, stirring. Add the tomatoes, rosemary, white wine and enough water to cover. Stew gently in a low oven until the meat is tender – 1½–2 hours depending on the age of the rabbit.

Remove the casserole from the oven and take out the meat with a slotted spoon. Boil the juices on top of the stove to reduce by half; then return to the meat and keep warm.

Roast the saddle fillets and the offal on a buttered baking tray in a very hot oven for 7 minutes only. Carve the fillets, liver and kidney very finely and serve with the casserole.

COMPOTE OF QUINCE WITH FROMAGE FRAIS

Serves 6

*12 quinces (2 per person)
sugar syrup made with half water, half sugar
fromage frais*

Chop half the quinces roughly, unpeeled and uncored. Cover with the sugar syrup and simmer for at least 1½ hours. The long simmering will eventually change the colour of the syrup from yellow through pink and red to almost brown. Stop simmering when you have the shade you prefer. Do not stir too often or too violently. Strain off the juice; do not press the fruit or the syrup will be cloudy. If it has reduced too much and is too sweet, dilute with water. Chill.

Peel and quarter the remaining quinces. Cut out the core and cut lengthways into slices about ¼ inch (0.5cm) thick. Poach in another half and half sugar syrup, removing them when just 'al dente'. Leave to cool.

Arrange the slices in a circle on individual plates, spoon over the dark syrup and add a blob of fromage frais.

Rosemary Glister

We have been at Bridgefield for ten years now, and over that period we have tried to develop a style and presentation that meets what we hope is public approval and also satisfies my way of cooking. This is to present food in as an attractive way as possible, but without covering up unduly the flavours, colours and textures that the food may have. To me it is just common sense to use fresh food in a way that brings out the best in the way of flavours and textures. A point in particular is the way vegetables are served in the vast majority of restaurants; overcooked and sauced. It is amazing the number of kind comments that come back to me in the kitchen about the fresh and attractive taste of the vegetables that we serve. There is such a vast variety of vegetables to be found in the shops today it really is surprising that more people do not experiment with them at home; and the golden rule is that they should never be overcooked. As an example, cabbage should be plunged into salted boiling water for three minutes then drained and served; done this way it is not only good for you but it tastes wonderful! What is really needed is a reappraisal of the attitude to vegetables in all forms, cooked and raw. If this was done perhaps the proliferation of frozen food firms and their wares would be halted and people would begin to enjoy their food at home more.

BLACK PUDDING IN A MUSTARD AND CREAM SAUCE

Serves 4

2 small shallots, thinly sliced
butter
3 large teaspoons wholegrain mustard
red wine
8 × ¼ inch (0.5cm) slices black pudding,
about 8 oz (225g)
salt and pepper

2½ fl oz (65ml) double cream
parsley, finely chopped

Our butcher (G. Denneys of Levens) makes his own black pudding in large, deep baking trays and then sells it either in pieces or slices. It is a totally different animal from the processed black puddings seen in supermarkets and delicatessens.

Fry the shallots in butter until golden and then add the mustard and red wine; simmer.

Cut the black pudding into small squares or chunks and either grill or put in the oven to heat through and remove some of the fat. Drain off the fat and add the black pudding to the shallots and wine. Return to the heat, reduce some of the liquid and season.

At the last minute, add the cream and cook for a further minute to allow the cream to mix with the wine. Serve in warmed dishes and sprinkle with finely chopped parsley.

POACHED SALMON ON A BED OF SAMPHIRE WITH A FRESH GINGER AND NOILLY PRAT SAUCE

Serves 4

4 fresh Scotch salmon steaks,
skin and bones removed
5 fl oz (150ml) Noilly Prat
1 oz (25g) fresh ginger, peeled and sliced
zest and juice of 2 oranges
2½ fl oz (60ml) double cream
a little butter
6 oz (175g) samphire

If samphire is unobtainable, finely sliced leeks may be used, but this is only a second best as the combination of the fish with the samphire is delicious.

Marinate the salmon in the Noilly Prat and sliced fresh ginger for 2 hours in the dish you are going to use for cooking. Add the juice and zest of the oranges and season. Cook the salmon for approximately 15 minutes in the oven at 375°F/190°C/Gas 5.

Strain the liquor from the fish, bring to the boil and reduce. Add the cream, taste and adjust the seasoning.

Break up the samphire and sauté in a little butter until heated through but not soft. Serve the salmon on a bed of the samphire and spoon over the sauce.

DAMSON FRUIT FOOL WITH ROSEMARY OR ANISE SHORTBREAD BISCUITS

Serves 4

1 egg white
2 tablespoons white sugar
5 fl oz (150ml) puréed and sieved damsons
5 fl oz (150ml) double cream

FOR THE SHORTBREAD

4 oz (125g) butter
2 oz (50g) sugar
6 oz (175g) flour
1–2 tablespoons fresh chopped rosemary
or dried anise

Whisk the egg white until dry and stiff, add the sugar and whisk again to resemble meringue. Whisk the cream to the same consistency and fold in the purée followed by the egg white. Pour into tall glasses, chill and serve with the biscuits.

To make the biscuits, combine all the ingredients in a food processor. Roll out, then cut out using a 2 inch (5cm) fluted cutter. Cook at 325°F/170°C/Gas 3 for 10–15 minutes. Sprinkle with caster sugar and cool. Keep the biscuits in an airtight tin.

Chris Grant

THE MANOR · CHADLINGTON

I had a degree in Physics and a career in Computer programming behind me before my husband and I went into the restaurant business ten years ago. Having run larger restaurants, we reached the conclusion that our style of cooking was at its best if we were serving a maximum of about twenty people. So the Manor at Chadlington was set up with this in mind. We serve of course only fresh food, and we are self-sufficient in herbs and vegetables which we grow in our own gardens. Our five-course menu changes daily according to what I have bought that day.

COURGETTE SOUFFLÉ WITH TOMATO SAUCE

Serves 8

2 tablespoons breadcrumbs
13 oz (375g) courgettes
4 tablespoons butter
1 onion, finely chopped
3 tablespoons plain flour
¾ cup milk
½ cup cream
pinch nutmeg
4 egg yolks
⅓ cup tasty cheese
3 tablespoons grated Parmesan
6 egg whites

Soufflés are never as difficult as they are made out to be.

Butter 8 ramekin dishes and sprinkle with breadcrumbs.

Wash and trim the courgettes and cook for a few minutes in boiling salted water until just tender. Then drain, chop and purée.

Melt the butter, soften the onion in it, add the flour and cook for 2 minutes. Add the milk, cream and courgette purée; season and add nutmeg. Remove from the heat and beat in the egg yolks and both cheeses. You can prepare in advance to this stage, then reheat gently when you are ready to serve, before folding in the whipped egg whites. Pour into the ramekins and sprinkle with a little extra Parmesan cheese. Cook at 400°F/200°C/Gas 6 for 12–15 minutes.

I serve this with a fresh tomato sauce.

SEA BASS WITH A HERB CRUST

Serves 4

1½ lbs (700g) sea bass, skinned and
filleted into 6oz (175g) pieces
4 tablespoons clarified butter
juice of half a lemon
5oz (150g) fine brioche crumbs
4oz (125g) finely chopped fresh herbs
(whatever you have)
1 tablespoon finely chopped parsley

Brush the fillets with clarified butter and add a little lemon juice. Grill under a preheated grill at a high heat for about 3 minutes on each side.

Meanwhile mix the brioche crumbs, herbs, parsley and a little salt and pepper, to get an even mixture. Spread this mixture over the fish, firming it down well. Then flash it under the grill in order to brown the herb crust. Serve the fish with a beurre blanc or Hollandaise sauce.

HAZELNUT MERINGUES WITH A RASPBERRY SAUCE

Serves 8

4½ oz (140g) hazelnuts
4 egg whites
9oz (250g) caster sugar
2 drops vanilla essence
½ teaspoon vinegar
cream and fresh raspberries, to serve

Brown the hazelnuts on a tray under the grill. Flake off most of the skins, then grind them in a blender to make ground hazelnuts.

Whisk the egg whites until stiff and gradually beat in the caster sugar. When very stiff, add the vanilla essence and vinegar. Fold in the ground hazelnuts. Put into a piping bag (a star shaped nozzle gives a nice shape) and pipe on to bakewell paper on a flat baking sheet. Bake at 350°F/180°C/Gas 4 for 30–40 minutes.

We serve these meringues with lots of cream and a fresh raspberry sauce made by puréeing raspberries with a little sugar, then pushing through a fine sieve to remove the pips.

Ruth Hadley

Scotland has a wonderful natural larder, and I am very fortunate at The Cross to have access to a major part of it. Venison, mountain hare and pigeon aplenty; wild salmon, seatrout and pike from crystal clear waters; halibut, turbot and seafood from the West Coast; I am even able to pick chanterelles and ceps in our immediate locality. All that plus incredible scenery and Highland hospitality! In the following recipes I would be drawing on this natural larder, the prawns would be king-sized fresh west coast prawns, but if these are not available to you good quality frozen prawns work just as well. The guineafowl we use are reared at Craufurdland Castle in Ayrshire, and I have been informed that they are becoming available through the major supermarkets. They taste similar to old fashioned chickens, rather than the new plastic (fishy) chickens we are becoming used to. Try to parcel the birds a day or two in advance and store in the fridge, as this gives the wine and cheeses time to flavour the meat. Although I can't claim that the pears in the tart are Scottish grown, I can tell you that Blairgowrie in Perthshire produces some of the finest raspberries in the world. The ever friendly David Pugh has supplied us with the freshest of fresh soft fruit since our earliest days.

PRAWN AND AVOCADO SALAD

Serves 4

5 fl oz (150ml) double cream, whipped until thick
2 tablespoons natural yoghurt
6 sprigs fresh basil
2 tomatoes, peeled, deseeded and diced
1 orange, segmented
1 lb (450g) cooked prawns (defrosted if frozen)
frisé lettuce
1 ripe avocado

Fold together the cream and yoghurt, then add 2 sprigs of basil, chopped, and the tomato flesh, orange segments and prawns. Season and chill.

To serve, arrange the prawn mixture on top of the frisé lettuce and garnish with slices of peeled avocado and the remaining sprigs of basil.

GUINEAFOWL PARCELS WITH BLUE CHEESE

Serves 4

4 oz (125g) cream cheese
4 oz (125g) blue cheese
1 sprig rosemary
2 x 2¼ lbs (1kg) fresh guineafowl (oven ready)
3 oz (75g) butter
chopped white of 1 leek
5 fl oz (150ml) white wine
seasoning

Blend together the two cheeses, adding a drop of milk if the mixture is too stiff. Chop the rosemary, add to the mixture and season.

Remove both halves of the guineafowls from their carcasses and cut off the wing tips. (Stock from the carcasses makes superb soups.) With each half of the bird, gently lift the skins of both the breast and thigh and stuff the cheese mixture between the skin and flesh. Fold the leg joint over the breast to form a neat round.

Take sufficient foil to form 4 parcels of *double* thickness, lay flat and butter the foil well. Divide the chopped leek into four and place in the centre of each piece of foil. Place the half guineafowl on top of the leeks and butter and season the fowl.

Turn up the corners of the foil and add a splash of wine. Fold the parcels securely and chill until ready to bake. Pre-heat the oven to 400°F/200°C/Gas 6 and bake the parcels for 40 – 45 minutes.

To serve, either open the parcels in the kitchen and transfer the contents on to warm plates, taking care not to spill the juices, or put the unopened parcel on the plate and allow your guests to open for themselves and catch the lovely aromas at the same time.

PEAR AND BUTTERSCOTCH TART

Serves 4 – 6

FOR THE PASTRY

3 oz (75g) butter
1 oz (25g) icing sugar
1 egg
6 oz (175g) plain flour

FOR THE FILLING

2 oz (50g) butter
5 oz (150g) light brown sugar
5 fl oz (150ml) double cream
2 egg yolks
3 ripe pears
lemon juice

To make the pastry, blend together the butter and sugar, add the egg and mix together. Add the flour, mix to a dough and chill until firm.

Roll out the pastry and use to line a well-greased 8½ inch (21.5cm) loose bottomed tart tin. Bake blind for 15 minutes at 375°F/190°C/Gas 5.

While the pastry is baking, make the filling. Melt the butter in a pan, stir in the sugar, heat to boiling point and stir in the cream. Lightly beat the egg yolks in a bowl, pour the hot sauce over them and then return it to the pan. Heat gently, stirring until the mixture thickens slightly but do not boil.

Peel, core and halve the pears and cut into slices. Arrange in the pastry case and brush with lemon juice. Pour over the butterscotch sauce and bake at 350°F/180°C/Gas 4 for 30–40 minutes until set. Leave to cool before serving.

For a more exotic taste, add the crushed seeds of 6 cardamom pods to the butterscotch sauce before baking.

Sue Harrison

We like to use fruits we collect from the surrounding countryside. We collect blackberries for the coulis served with the Hazelnut Parfait, crab-apples to make jelly to serve with game, and also to make the butter which we serve with Normandy Apple Flan and whortleberries which we collect from the moor (when we have time!) to be made into ice cream and served with our own rosehip syrup. Chris, my husband, also makes sloe gin, blackberry brandy, and elderberry wine (a prizewinner at our local Flower and Veg Show!) which I use in many dishes.

TIMBALE OF BROCCOLI

Serves 2

6 oz (175g) broccoli
1 egg
1 – 2 fl oz (25 – 50ml) double cream
salt and pepper
fresh tomato sauce, chopped basil and warm shallot vinaigrette, to serve

FOR THE VINAIGRETTE
½ shallot, very finely chopped
3 fl oz (75ml) olive oil
salt and pepper
little lemon juice

Preheat the oven to 400°F/200°C/Gas 6. Cook the broccoli in boiling salted water, cool and then squeeze out excess moisture. Place in a food processor with sufficient egg and cream to process to a smooth purée – the mixture should not be too wet. Season.

Oil 2 dariole moulds, place a circle of greaseproof paper at the bottom of each and pour in the mousse. Cover with buttered foil and poach in a bain-marie filled with boiling water in the oven for about 20 minutes until firm to the touch.

Meanwhile make the vinaigrette. Cook the shallot in a little of the oil, then add the remaining oil and season with salt, pepper and lemon juice to taste. Warm the pan very gently on the side of the stove (not over direct heat) to allow the flavours to infuse.

When the timbales are cooked, turn each into the centre of a plate, surround with an inner circle of fresh tomato sauce and an outer circle of warm shallot vinaigrette, sprinkle with chopped basil and serve.

BONED QUAIL STUFFED WITH WILD RICE AND APRICOTS

Serves 2

1 small onion, finely chopped
butter
1 oz (25g) cooked wild rice
5 dried apricots,
soaked for a few hours and finely chopped
fresh parsley and thyme
4 boned quail (use the bones to make a stock)

FOR THE SAUCE

1 oz (25g) granulated sugar
1 tablespoon vinegar
¼ pint (150ml) stock (made from the bones)
juice and rind of 1 large orange
1 dessertspoon Cointreau
1 oz (25g) butter
orange segments, to decorate

Preheat the oven to 400°F/200°C/Gas 6. Cook the chopped onion in butter until soft and mix with the rice, apricots and herbs. Season and enclose the stuffing in the quail, securing each with a cocktail stick. Cook in the hot oven for 20 –25 minutes.

Meanwhile make the sauce. Place the sugar and vinegar in a heavy saucepan and caramelise over a gentle heat. Add the stock, stirring to dissolve the caramel. Add the orange juice and rind, and the Cointreau and reduce a little.

Remove the quail and add the sauce to the cooking dish, stirring to pick up any caramelised pieces in the bottom; reduce again if necessary. Whisk in the butter over a gentle heat – do not allow to boil. Spoon the sauce over the quail and decorate with orange segments.

PRALINE PARFAIT

Serves 12

7 oz (200g) caster sugar
1 oz (25g) hazelnuts
4 eggs, separated
½ teaspooon vanilla essence
½ pint (275ml) double cream

FOR THE BLACKBERRY COULIS

8 oz (225g) blackberries
5 oz (150g) caster sugar
lemon juice
whole blackberries and mint leaves, to decorate

Melt 2 oz (50g) sugar to a dark caramel and add the hazelnuts. Mix well, place on an oiled tray and allow to cool. Place briefly in the food processor, but don't grind too finely.

Beat the egg yolks with 3 oz (75g) of the sugar and vanilla essence until thick. Add the ground hazelnuts and fold in the double cream. Beat the egg whites with the remaining 2 oz (50g) sugar until stiff and fold carefully into the mixture. Line a 3 pint (1.75 litre) loaf tin with clingfilm, pour in the mixture and freeze.

To make the coulis, liquidise the blackberries with the sugar and lemon juice to taste. Sieve and chill before serving. To serve, place a slice of the parfait on the coulis decorated with whole blackberries and mint leaves.

Nicola Hayward

SEAVIEW HOTEL · ISLE OF WIGHT

I was born and brought up on the Island. I love it dearly and think it has much to offer. When we bought the Seaview Hotel, supplies were difficult. I worked very closely with three local fishermen and a farmer from the centre of the Island. I take whatever the fishermen catch; my view is that a fresh plaice is better than frozen scampi. Consequently we have a varied selection every day. Shell fish is always available – weather permitting – but sadly sea bass which was abundant here ten years ago is becoming rare. The farmer, Colin Boswell of Mersley Farms, is an exceptional man. He recently won an award for exporting local garlic to France! He also produces wonderful local asparagus, baby carrots, new potatoes, baby sweetcorn, delicious shallots and calabrese. The pheasants are all local as are the pigeon breasts, venison and lamb I use in the restaurant. I always use fresh herbs, which I grow myself. We also use local fruit, particularly strawberries and raspberries which we serve with Island cream.

HOT CRAB RAMEKIN

Serves 4 – 6

1 lb (450g) crab meat, freshly picked if possible
and drained of any liquid
1 cup thick double cream
4 oz (125g) grated cheese
pinch dried mustard powder or mace
lemon juice
anchovy essence
chilli sauce
freshly ground pepper and salt

To make the mixture less rich, a cheese sauce may be used instead of cream. The mixture may be made in advance and heated in the oven or microwave before browning.

Mix the cream and crab meat together over a gentle heat. Add half the grated cheese together with all the other ingredients and cook until hot. Pour into ramekin dishes and sprinkle with the remaining grated cheese. Brown under the grill or in a hot oven.

BREAST OF PHEASANT WITH APPLE AND PINK PEPPERCORN COMPOTE

Serves 4

4 breasts of pheasant (2 birds and trimmings)
butter
oil
few sprigs fresh rosemary
freshly ground black pepper and salt
2 large cooking apples
pink peppercorns
lemon juice

Either bone out the pheasant breasts yourself or get your butcher to do it for you. Boil up the carcasses and legs and make stock.

Lightly seal the breasts in a pan with a little butter, oil, a sprig of fresh rosemary and pepper and salt. Wrap each breast in tin foil with another sprig of rosemary and set aside.

Peel and dice the apples, add a few pink peppercorns and lightly heat with a few drops of lemon juice until mushy. Keep the sauce warm.

Place the breasts in a hot oven 425°F/220°C/ Gas 7 for 20 minutes. Reduce the pheasant stock right down until syrup-like. Place each breast on a plate and slice thinly. Pour over a little of the reduced stock and a spoonful of the apple compote. Serve immediately.

MERINGUES WITH PASSION FRUIT AND ORANGES

Serves 4 – 6

2 egg whites
4 oz (125g) caster sugar
2 oz (50g) honey
lemon juice
6 passion fruit
4 large oranges, peeled and segmented
with pith and skin removed
whipped cream

Beat the egg whites until stiff, slowly beat in 2 oz (50g) sugar and then fold in the remainder. Using 2 tablespoons, shape the meringue mixture into small ovals. Place in grease-proofed trays and bake for 1 hour at 275°F/ 140°C/Gas 1.

Boil the honey with a little water and a squeeze of lemon juice until a syrup. Add the passion fruit and orange segments. Place 2 meringues on a plate and pipe a swirl of whipped cream over them. Pour the sauce around and serve immediately.

Catherine Healy

We had to establish our own garden to grow fresh herbs, unusual vegetables and salads, since it was impossible to obtain a reliable supply locally. Most of the meat and game we use in the restaurant comes from local suppliers of which an increasing number are free range and organic. It has always been our policy to encourage small local producers and this seems to be a pronounced trend all over the country so that the quality of raw materials is improving all the time.

MOUSSE OF KOHL RABI

Serves 6

8 oz (225g) peeled kohl rabi
2 oz (50g) butter
1 pint (570ml) cream
4 leaves gelatine
mixed salad leaves, for garnish

Chop the kohl rabi into small pieces. Melt the butter in a heavy saucepan, add the kohl rabi and cook very gently, covered, until soft. Pour in the cream and bring to the boil.

Soak the gelatine leaves in cold water until soft. Liquidise the kohl rabi and cream until really smooth. Season to taste and add the softened gelatine. Mix very well and pour into individual oiled moulds. Leave to set in the fridge.

To serve, turn out on to small plates garnished with mixed salad leaves.

BREAST OF PIGEON WITH RED CHARD, SAUCE BEAUJOLAIS

Serves 6

6 plump pigeons
6 leaves red chard
½ bottle Beaujolais
1 teaspoon balsamic vinegar
a little butter

Draw and clean the pigeons. Remove the breasts and make a good stock from the carcases – this may be done the day before.

Blanch the chard leaves and keep in iced water until ready to serve. Strain the pigeon stock and add the red wine. Simmer until the sauce is of a good consistency, add the balsamic vinegar and cook for a further few minutes – whisk in a little butter and keep warm until ready to serve.

Lightly cook the pigeon breasts and arrange on the warmed chard leaves. Pour over the sauce and serve immediately.

COMPOTE OF SUMMER FRUIT WITH ELDERFLOWER SYRUP

Serves 12

4 lbs (1.8kg) mixed summer fruit
2 pints (1.1 litres) elderflowers
1 lb (450g) sugar
2 pints (1.1 litres) water

Prepare and wash the fruit. Place in a large heatproof bowl and set aside.

Wash the elderflowers and place in a saucepan with the sugar and water. Bring slowly to the boil and simmer gently for 15 minutes. Strain the syrup into another saucepan, bring it back to boiling point and pour it quickly over the mixed fruit – the boiling syrup will partially cook it.

Leave for 24 hours before serving – this allows the flavours of the fruit to infuse.

Patricia Hegarty

HOPE END · LEDBURY

Hope End, which celebrated its tenth anniversary in 1989, was founded on the belief that good wholesome, seasonal, local English food, a catch phrase now on the lips of half the restaurants in England, was the best recipe for a country hotel, at a time when 'French cuisine' ruled.
We grow an extraordinary range of fruit, vegetables and herbs in our eighteenth century walled garden. We also use eggs from free range hens and exceptional local beef, lamb and fish and game in season. There is always fresh homemade brown bread; a selection of rare English farmhouse cheeses is usually available and the hotel has its own fine spring water.

LOVAGE SOUFFLÉ

Serves 6 – 8

3 oz (75g) brown breadcrumbs
bunch fresh lovage sprigs, to taste
1 oz (25g) unsalted butter, plus extra for greasing
1 oz (25g) wholemeal flour
½ pint (275ml) milk
5 large eggs, separated
2 tablespoons grated Parmesan
sea salt
black pepper

Lovage is an extremely vigorous herb shooting up from nothing to an enormous bush 8 or 9 feet high in the space of a few months. The same strength is characteristic of the flavour of its dark glossy leaves, which permeates the light bulk of a soufflé beautifully.

Preheat the oven to 425°F/220°C/Gas 7. Butter 6–8 individual ramekins and line them with breadcrumbs, shaking out the excess. Keep the remainder of the breadcrumbs for the tops.

Strip the lovage leaves into small pieces and soften them in melted butter. Stir in the flour and gradually add the milk to make a sauce. Whizz the sauce in a liquidiser until flecked green. Cool, then incorporate the egg yolks, 1 tablespoon of the Parmesan and the seasoning. The mixture will be fairly runny.

Whip the egg whites until stiff, fold them into the soufflé sauce base and fill the ramekins loosely level. Mix the remaining breadcrumbs and Parmesan together and sprinkle over the top.

Bake in the preheated oven for 10 minutes or until the soufflés are nicely risen and still slightly moist in the middle.

HEREFORD BEEF FILLET IN MUSTARD AND SAVORY SAUCE

Serves 6

2 lbs (900g) fillet steak
handful winter savory sprigs
1 tablespoon olive oil
3 teaspoons English mustard made up with water
6 teaspoons cider vinegar
6 fl oz (175ml) double cream
sea salt
black pepper

We are extremely lucky in having two family butchers in Ledbury who have beautifully hung and flavoursome beef – as it should be in this countryside famous for its Hereford cattle. Winter Savory is being rediscovered; it is an old established herb in English cooking with evergreen type leaves. Its strong taste stands up to beef particularly well.

Cut the steak into strips about 2 inches (5cm) by ¼ inch (0.5cm). Chop the savory leaves very finely, reserving a few for decoration. Heat the oil in a heavy frying pan, sear the meat and cook it briefly. Remove the meat, cover and keep it warm.

Stir the rest of the ingredients into the frying pan and reduce the sauce. Turn the strips of meat in the sauce and serve, or alternatively arrange the strips in the centre of each plate surrounded by the sauce and decorated with very small sprigs of savory.

RHUBARB BRÛLÉE

Serves 6

1 lb (450g) prepared rhubarb
3 tablespoons water
few sweet cicely leaves
4 tablespoons demerera sugar,
or to taste

FOR THE CUSTARD

4 free range egg yolks
3 tablespoons demerera sugar, plus extra to glaze
½ pint (275ml) double cream
vanilla pod or ½ teaspoon natural vanilla essence

Fruit brûlées work best with really vibrant tasting fruit such as damsons, raspberries and rhubarb which cut across the sweetness of the sugar glaze and the smoothness of the custard. The sweet cicely leaves help allay some of the sharpness of the rhubarb so that less sugar is needed.

Trim the rhubarb sticks and cut into 1 inch (2.5cm) lengths. Soften these slowly in a stainless steel pan with the water and sweet cicely leaves. Remove the leaves and add the minimum of sugar to be palatable. Tip into a shallow fireproof dish.

Make the custard by whipping the egg yolks and sugar together. Heat the cream with the vanilla pod and pour over the eggs and sugar. Return the mixture to the saucepan and stir well until it thickens without boiling. Sieve the custard and spoon it over the rhubarb.

When cool, chill in the refrigerator. Turn on the grill to half. Cover the custard with a layer of demerera sugar and glaze under the grill. Watch carefully to see that it does not burn, though one or two darker patches positively help it live up to its name – 'burnt cream'! The top will set into a brittle sheet of caramel when it has cooled and should stay hard for a few hours if it is not in too steamy an atmosphere.

Angela Hewitt

LUGLEYS RESTAURANT · ISLE OF WIGHT

It is ten years since I opened Lugleys. Since those early days I have developed a greed for perfection. It started in my second year when I obtained a mention in the Egon Ronay Guide for good cooking. There it was in black and white, a small entry of encouragement. I was naturally thrilled to be noticed, to be set apart from other eating places. I visited other mentioned establishments, mainly with star ratings to discover the standard of cuisine they offered. Most noticeable was their emphasis on quality and not quantity, either in the food served or the long lists of reading beforehand. My approach to food changed virtually overnight as I realised what excellence really meant. It meant wobbly jellies, succulent chicken breasts, fresh, opaque fish, melting mousses and tender loving care.

I knew that with a choice of twelve starters, fifteen main dishes and a dozen puddings I was not going to achieve my new goal. Yet I could not change my menu overnight. It took all of eight years to slowly and cautiously pluck from the menu the range of dishes I carried, to now, with the choice of three dishes I offer at each course.

I now produce a very small regularly changing seasonal menu which suits the capabilities of a solo cook such as myself with no formal teaching. My two favourite seasons are Summer and Autumn. Summer induces a desire for Mediterranean sunshine foods: peppers, tomatoes, basil, lobsters, salads, pasta, oils and luscious soft fruits. It is also time to make my preserves. Redcurrant jelly, gooseberry and mint jelly, quince jelly and spiced peaches. Autumn brings the onset of game, starting with Highland grouse in August. The Game Season is a most enjoyable and satisfying time to cook. Wild food it appears, demands a respect other foods do not and I tend to treat these untamed foods to a regality not shared with domesticated breeds. Even the food I bring from home, my muscovy eggs and meat, my home grown herbs and fruits, I revere, in comparison with anything that I may buy from my suppliers.

NUGGETS OF SALMON AND ROULADE OF COD WITH SORREL AND ORANGE SAUCES

Serves 4

2 large or 4 small cod fillets, about 1 lb (450 g)
4 sheets filo pastry
2 oz (50g) butter, melted
sprigs fresh, delicate herbs (dill, fennel, chervil)
seasoning
1 lb (450g) centre salmon fillet
2 oz (50g) butter
herbs (as above)

FOR THE SORREL SAUCE

2 shallots, finely chopped
2 tablespoons oil
½ pint (275ml) white wine
5 fl oz (150ml) fish stock
about 8 sorrel leaves, shredded
6 fl oz (175ml) double cream
seasoning

FOR THE ORANGE SAUCE

2 shallots, finely chopped
2 tablespoons oil
½ pint (275ml) fresh orange juice
1 teaspoon honey
5 fl oz (150ml) fish stock
6 fl oz (175ml) double cream
seasoning

First make the sorrel sauce (do not use an aluminium pan). Soften the shallots in the oil without colouring. Add the wine and stock and reduce to about 5 fl oz (150ml). Add the shredded sorrel leaves and the cream. Bring to the boil and simmer for 4 – 5 minutes. Process until very smooth, season to taste and strain. Place in an ovenproof bowl and set aside.

Follow the same procedure for the orange sauce replacing the white wine with the orange juice, add 1 teaspoon honey and omit the sorrel.

If you are using 2 large cod fillets, cut them in half lengthways. Brush each sheet of filo with melted butter and fold in two. Lay a cod fillet diagonally across each pastry square. Scatter the herbs over the fish and smear liberally with melted butter. Fold a corner of the pastry over the fish and roll up into a flat tube shape. Now wind this tube into a coil, sealing the end with melted butter. Brush with more butter or beaten egg and place on a baking tray.

Skin the salmon fillet and cut it across into 4 pieces. With the skinned side on the outside, fold up into a nugget shape whereby the thin end meets up with the thick end. Secure with a greased cocktail stick. Arrange the nuggets on a liberally buttered ovenproof plate. Lay a sprig of herb and a dot of butter on each nugget and cover with foil.

Reheat the two sauces in a microwave.

Preheat the oven to 425°F/220°C/Gas 7. Put the 2 bowls of sauce in a roasting pan filled with hot water. Cover the bowls with foil and place the pan in the bottom of the oven to keep warm. Place the cod roulades at the top of the oven and bake for 15 minutes. Cook the salmon at the bottom of the oven for 15 minutes (10 minutes if you have a fan oven).

To serve, pour a small amount of each sauce on each plate. Arrange the cod on the orange sauce and the salmon on the sorrel sauce.

RAGOUT OF CALVES SWEETBREADS WITH RED VERMOUTH AND CURRANT SAUCE

Serves 4

1 lb (450g) calves sweetbreads
2 bay leaves
2 cloves garlic
1 onion
1 carrot
2 – 3 sticks salsify
8 baby carrots
seasoned flour
oil for frying

FOR THE SAUCE

1 onion, finely shredded
8 pickling onions or small shallots
½ pint (275ml) red vermouth
½ pint (275ml) jellied beef stock
1 tablespoon honey
2 tablespoons vinegar
2 tablespoons dark soya sauce or Tamari
2 oz (50g) currants
6 oz (175g) butter, diced

Place the sweetbreads in a bowl of heavily salted water and stand for 3 – 4 hours. Drain and rinse well. Place in a saucepan of fresh cold water, bring to the boil and remove any scum that rises to the surface. Add the bay leaf, garlic, onion and carrot. Reduce the heat and simmer for 30 minutes. Remove from the heat and set aside until ready to use.

Thinly peel the salsify and cut into 1 inch (2.5cm) lengths. Cook in boiling water with a slice of lemon or dash of vinegar until *al dente*. Drain. Turn the carrots into small, dainty carrot shapes. Boil until *al dente* and drain. Peel the small onions and keep whole.

To make the sauce, soften the sliced onions with the whole onions in oil until golden. Add all the remaining sauce ingredients except the butter, simmer rapidly and reduce to a scant ½ pint (275ml). Put aside. The dish can be prepared up to this point the day before.

Drain the sweetbreads and remove any excess pieces of fat. Break into bite-sized pieces. Toss lightly in seasoned flour. Pan fry in hot oil until golden brown and very crisp on the outside. Keep warm while finishing the dish. Add the small carrots and salsify to the sauce and reheat. When boiling, whisk in the butter to make a smooth, velvety sauce. Arrange the sweetbreads, vegetables and sauce on warm plates and serve immediately.

APPLE, BLACKBERRY AND LAVENDER FLOWER MERINGUE WITH ROSE PETAL ICE CREAM

Serves 4

FOR THE ICE CREAM

3 large eggs, separated
6 oz (175g) caster sugar
1 tablespoon triple distilled rosewater
few drops cochineal colouring
1 pint (570ml) double cream
few dried rosepetals, crumbled (optional)

FOR THE LAVENDER SUGAR

1 pint (570ml) lavender flower heads
1 lb (450g) caster sugar
1 lb (450g) powdered glucose

1 lb (450g) cooking apples
4 oz (125g) caster sugar
8 oz (225g) blackberries
3 egg whites

To make the ice cream, whisk the egg yolks with half the sugar over hot water until thick and creamy. Whisk in the rosewater and about ¼ teaspoon colouring. Allow to cool. Whip the cream into soft peaks. Whisk the egg whites with the remaining sugar to soft peaks. Carefully fold the cream into the cooled yolk mixture, then the egg whites and rose petals, if used. Freeze in a plastic container overnight.

Transfer from the freezer to the fridge 30 minutes before serving.

To make the lavender sugar, put the flower heads in a low oven or microwave to dry. Mix together the 2 sugars, add to the flower heads and whiz in a blender until as fine a powder as possible. Keep in an airtight container until ready to use. This quantity will be sufficient for several recipes.

Peel and slice the apples and place in a pan with the caster sugar. Stew gently until soft but not pulpy. Add the blackberries for the last few minutes. Turn the mixture into individual ramekins.

Whisk the egg whites until very stiff and dry. Whisk in 6 oz (175g) of the lavender sugar. Continue whisking until the meringue is firm and glossy. Spread the meringue over the fruit in peaks, sealing the edges. Flash under a preheated grill for a few seconds only to brown. Serve immediately with a small dish of the ice cream.

Baba Hine

I have spent the last 20 years cooking and running my own kitchens for numbers over 50 per night; firstly for 8 years at our hotel in Wales, and for the past 12 years here at Corse Lawn. I have enjoyed considerable success, gaining a first AA Rosette in 1970, a Good Food Guide 'Pestle and Mortar' in 1975, and an Egon Ronay Star in 1979, and more recently an Ackerman Four Leaf Clover in 1989. To keep such high standards over the years, I have listed some of the most important strengths one needs. Not in any particular order, they are:- Flair (born, not made); strength; ambition; determination; a talented supporting team; and loyal suppliers; with an unfailing sense of humour!

HOT SHRIMPS EN CROUSTADE

Serves 4 – 6

1 lb (450g) peeled brown shrimps
2 tablespoons finely chopped shallots
1 tablespoon finely chopped parsley
1 large teaspoon finely chopped thyme
1 large teaspoon finely chopped tarragon
1 pinch saffron
salt and pepper
2 oz (50g) butter
2 oz (50g) flour
5 fl oz (150ml) white wine
½ pint (275ml) fish stock
2 oz (50g) fresh tomato purée
1 tablespoon brandy
½ pint (275ml) double cream
small pastry cases made with ½ lb (225g) shortcrust pastry

Sauté 1 oz (25g) of the shrimps with the shallots, herbs and seasoning in the butter until light gold. Add the flour, then the white wine, fish stock, tomato purée and brandy. Cook for about 10 minutes. Add the cream and the rest of the shrimps and remove from the heat.

Bake very thin shortcrust pastry baskets separately. Pour the shrimp mixture into the warm pastry cases and serve.

PIGEON BREASTS WITH WILD MUSHROOM MOUSSE AND RED WINE

Serves 6

FOR THE MOUSSE

6 oz (175g) wild mushrooms
2 oz (50g) butter
salt and pepper
6 egg whites
6 fl oz (175ml) cream

9 pigeons
2 oz (50g) butter
3 oz (75g) wild mushrooms, sliced
2 fl oz (50ml) red wine

To make the mousse, sauté the wild mushrooms (trompette de mort, girolles, shitake, pied de mouton, pleurotes etc) in the butter with salt and pepper to taste, until light brown, allow to cool. Blend in a liquidiser until smooth then fold in the cream and beaten egg whites. Pour into individual buttered moulds and poach until set, covered with foil, in a bain-marie at 400°F/200°C/Gas 6 for 12 minutes.

Meanwhile remove the breasts from the pigeons. Make a stock with the carcasses. Sauté the pigeon breasts in the butter for just a couple of minutes until pink, then leave to rest. Add the wild mushrooms to the pan juices and lightly brown. Add the red wine and a little of the pigeon stock and reduce by half. Season to taste.

To serve, turn out the warm mousse on to the centre of the plate. Pour the sauce and mushrooms around. Slice each breast into 3 thin slices, position on the plate and serve.

STRAWBERRY COLLECTION

Serves 6

FOR THE ICED SOUFFLÉ

3 egg whites
4 oz (125g) sugar
½ lb (225g) strawberries
1 tablespoon kirsch
5 fl oz (150ml) cream

FOR THE SORBET

7 oz (200g) sugar
½ pint (275ml) water
½ lb (225g) strawberries

FOR THE COULIS

½ lb (225g) strawberries
3½ oz (100g) sugar

small shortcake biscuits, tiny almond tuiles and caramel cages, to serve
½ lb (225g) strawberries, quartered, to decorate

To make the soufflé, whisk the egg whites and sugar over a sharp heat until double in size and very hot. Then place in a mixer and whisk until cool and firm. Meanwhile liquidise the strawberries and kirsch. Fold into the meringue mixture, then fold in the cream. Pour into individual containers and freeze.

To make the sorbet, heat the sugar and water until boiling and allow to cool. Liquidise the strawberries and add to the cooled syrup. Freeze.

To make the coulis beat together the strawberries and sugar, then pass through a sieve.

To assemble, turn out the soufflé on to the side of the plate. Place a quenelle of sorbet in a tuile covered by a caramel cage at a 45° angle on the other side of the plate. Put a small shortcake decorated with strawberry quarters and dusted with icing sugar at the top of the triangle and pour a little strawberry coulis in the centre.

Long on preparation, but worth it!

Ros Hunter

THE VILLAGE RESTAURANT · RAMSBOTTOM

Before we had any professional connection with catering, my husband, Chris Johnson and I both used to dine out frequently. Several restaurants that we particularly enjoyed for the quality and value of their food offered limited choice menus, served at a set time. Most were small, friendly places, run personally by the proprietors. Some of the least memorable dishes (and all of the most expensive meals), were from à la carte menus!

Five years ago, when we decided to open a restaurant of our own, we felt that our best chance of success would be to stick to the extended dinner party formula which we had enjoyed at La Potinière, Miller Howe, Sharrow Bay etc. This proved to have many advantages in a new restaurant, where business was not predictable, and often non existent!

A year after we started Chris happened to find George Cooper, a wonderful organic market gardener who supplies us with perfect vegetables, fruits, herbs and salads, and has introduced us to other organic growers who provide meats, dairy produce etc. The quality of our fresh salads and vegetables proves that the flavour and texture of produce grown in a natural, chemical free agricultural system, is incomparable.

FENNEL SOUP

Serves 12

12 oz (350g) onions, skinned and chopped
6 oz (175g) butter
3 lbs (1.4kg) fennel, cut into even pieces
freshly ground black pepper
2½ pints (1.4 litres) good strong chicken stock
up to 1 pint (570ml) whipping cream
fennel tops or ground paprika for garnish

Cook the onions in the butter over a low heat until transparent. Raise the heat, add the fennel, ½ pint (275ml) of the chicken stock and lots of pepper. Cover and steam until the fennel softens. Add the rest of the stock, cover and simmer gently for 1 hour. Cool and put through a food processor to make a thick purée. At this stage you can pass the soup through a fine sieve – I prefer not to, as it tends to lose 'body'.

Bring the purée to the boil in a clean pan. Adjust the seasoning to taste. Lower the heat and just prior to serving, add cream to make a fairly thick soup. Garnish.

POACHED SALMON WITH HERB AND CUCUMBER MAYONNAISE

Serves 12

very fresh 7 – 8 lb (2.5 – 3kg)
salmon, gutted and thoroughly cleaned
organic salad leaves
(lettuce, sorrel, baby spinach etc)

FOR THE COURT BOUILLON
hot water
3 fl oz (75ml) white wine vinegar
small handful chopped fresh or dried herbs
(chervil, thyme, basil, French tarragon)
6 bay leaves
2 medium onions, roughly chopped (leave skins on)
small handful whole black peppercorns
scant dessertspoon sea salt

FOR THE HERB AND CUCUMBER MAYONNAISE
2 eggs
14 fl oz (375ml) refined sunflower oil
1 tablespoon good Dijon mustard
3 heaped tablespoons finely chopped
mixed fresh herbs
1 dessertspoon tarragon or dill vinegar
freshly ground black pepper
1 cucumber, finely diced
edible flowers, to garnish

To make your court bouillon, fill a 24 inch fish kettle two-thirds full with hot water. Add the vinegar, herbs, onions, pepper and salt. Bring to the boil and simmer for 5 minutes.

Gently lower the fish into the court bouillon – it should be just covered – quickly bring back to the boil, then put the lid on the fish kettle, reduce the heat and simmer for 6 minutes. Turn the heat off and leave to cool overnight. This ensures that the salmon is moist and delicate.

An hour or so before your guests arrive, take the salmon out of the court bouillon, carefully remove the skin and dark meat and ease the flesh from the bones. Break into portions and place each on a bed of salad leaves.

To make the mayonnaise, break the eggs into a food processor. With the motor running, slowly add the sunflower oil. When the mixture has thickened, add the vinegar, mustard, pepper and chopped herbs (the flavour is better if you match the vinegar to one of the fresh herbs). Just prior to serving, fold in the cucumber, spoon over the salmon and garnish with edible flowers (e.g. borage, Aaron's Rod, viola).

LANCASHIRE 'WET NELLIE'

Serves 12

6 oz (175g) dried vine fruits
1 wine glass Malmsey Madeira
12 oz (350g) plain Madeira cake
zest of 3 lemons, juice of 2
6 fl oz (175ml) whipping cream
1 x 10 inch (25cm) sweet pastry shell,
lightly cooked (I use pâte sucrée)
freshly soured cream, stirred with
a pinch of cinnamon, to serve

This is an adaptation of a pudding said to have been enjoyed by Lord Nelson! It is very rich so serve fairly small portions.

Soak the fruit in the Madeira for a couple of days until completely absorbed. Break the cake into fine crumbs and combine with the fruit, lemon juice and zest and cream to make a sticky mixture. Spoon into the pastry shell and bake at 350°F/180°C/Gas 4 for about 40 minutes until light golden. Serve warm. Freshly soured cream spiked with ground cinnamon counteracts the richness rather well.

Margaret Jackson

REEDS · POUGHILL

I have not had any professional training but my love for entertaining for family occasions led me to buy this Edwardian house in a beautiful garden and run it as a country house hotel – I was awarded a Cesar in the Good Hotel Guide for 1990. I only use the finest and freshest ingredients and do not take short cuts. My fishmonger, Alf Flowa, goes daily to Bideford for fresh fish and I can buy an excellent selection of cheeses from 'Simple Life', a delicatessen in Bude. Free-range eggs come from my son-in-law's farm and meat is supplied by Russells of Exeter. I always make a point of asking guests about food preferences so that I can produce dishes which they will enjoy.

TOMATO ICE CREAM

Serves 6

FOR THE MAYONNAISE
1 egg
1 tablespoon lemon juice
salt, pepper and mustard, to taste
8 – 10 fl oz (225 – 275ml) olive or sunflower oil

1 lb (450g) tomatoes
1 clove garlic, chopped
2 – 3 bay leaves
small bunch fresh herbs
(e.g. basil, marjoram, parsley or tarragon)
1 teaspoon tomato purée if necessary
juice of 1 lemon
grated zest of 1 orange
3 fl oz (75ml) partially whipped cream
salt and pepper to taste

sliced avocado and whole prawns, to decorate

First make the mayonnaise. Blend the egg, lemon juice and seasoning until well mixed. Slowly add the oil, with the blender at a low speed until a thick mixture is obtained. The amount of oil may vary according to the size of the egg.

Stew the tomatoes with the garlic, bay leaves and fresh herbs until soft (about 15 minutes). Allow to cool a little, then sieve to make ½ pint (275ml) tomato pulp, adding the tomato purée for added richness if necessary.

Gently mix the mayonnaise with the tomato mixture, then incorporate the other ingredients in the order given. Taste, adjust for seasoning and freeze. Allow to mellow for 1 hour in the refrigerator before serving. Decorate with slices of avocado, prawns and extra mayonnaise sharpened with tabasco and tomato purée.

PAUPIETTES OF SOLE WITH SMOKED SALMON IN A WHITE WINE SAUCE

Serves 4

12 paupiettes of sole or lemon sole
2 oz (50g) smoked salmon
1 oz (25g) butter
squeeze lemon juice
pinch black pepper
white wine
a little milk
mixed fresh herbs as available
pinch mace
a little flour
4 oz (125g) mushrooms

Pound the smoked salmon with the butter, lemon juice and black pepper. Spread a little of the smoked salmon mixture on to each paupiette and roll up, skin side uppermost. Place in a buttered ovenproof dish and partially cover with the wine. Cover and poach in the oven for 10 minutes at 375°F/190°C/Gas 5.

Remove the fillets from the wine and leave to drain, reserving the juice. Infuse the milk with a pinch of mace and fresh herbs. Make a sauce using the butter, flour, the reserved fish stock and the infused milk. Enrich with cream if liked. Chop the mushrooms and sweat in a little butter. Place the fish on a bed of the mushrooms, cover with the sauce and heat in the oven at 350°F/180°C/Gas 4 until bubbling.

SNOW CHEESE

Serves 6

4 oz (125g) caster sugar
rind and juice of 1 large lemon
15 fl oz (400ml) double cream
2 egg whites
whipped cream, fresh fruit salad and
Grand Marnier, to serve

Stir the sugar and the rind and juice of the lemon into the cream. Beat carefully until thick and incorporate the stiffly beaten egg whites. Pour into a sieve lined with damp muslin and place over a bowl to drain for at least 24 hours. Turn out on to a flat dish, peel off the muslin and decorate with rosettes of cream. Serve with a salad of fresh fruits (not grapefruit) laced with Grand Marnier.

Marion Jones

Ours is a small restaurant in an old Victorian bakery, set on the side of the Malvern Hills. I cook and my husband, Robin, waits. We have no staff. Also I grow in our own garden vegetables, Alpine strawberries and many herbs, which we use in profusion. We opened in 1978 and, among other awards, have been awarded a Michelin star each year since 1981.

SOUP OF CAULIFLOWER, LEEK AND DILL

Serves 8

6 small leeks (shred a little for garnish)
1 large onion, finely sliced
1 oz (25g) butter
3 pints (1.75 litres) light stock
3 large, firm white cauliflowers
(cut small florets for garnish from half of one)
1 medium potato, finely sliced
1 bunch dill (reserve a little for garnish)
1 fl oz (25ml) double cream
seasoning

Soften the leek and onion in butter in a large saucepan. Cut the cauliflowers into pieces and add them to the saucepan together with the stock and potato. Cook until tender. Blend until smooth with the chopped dill. To serve, reheat, adjust the consistency with more stock, add the cream, season and add the cauliflower florets (previously cooked briefly in salted water). Serve garnished with the reserved dill and leeks.

LAMB AS VENISON WITH PARSNIP, WILD RICE AND WOODRUFF

Serves 8

FOR THE MARINADE

2½ fl oz (65ml) olive oil
1 small carrot, ½ onion, 1 stick celery, finely sliced
½ bottle full-bodied red wine
1 tablespoon red wine vinegar
½ teaspoon salt
10 peppercorns
1 clove
4 crushed juniper berries
1 bay leaf
1 sprig rosemary

mature leg of lamb, about 5 lb (2.3g),
outside trimmed, boned out but not tunnel boned

FOR THE STUFFING

a little olive oil or butter
2 lbs (900g) parsnips, peeled, quartered and cored
1 small onion, chopped
1 clove garlic, chopped
2½ oz (65g) wild rice,
cooked according to packet instructions
small bunch woodruff
(use rosemary if unobtainable)

few slices onion, carrot, celery
3 tablespoons port
reduced stock made from chopped,
browned lamb bones
pared lemon rind
½ stick cinnamon
1 tablespoon redcurrant jelly

Make the marinade by sweating the vegetables in oil for 10 minutes, add the wine and spices and simmer for 15 minutes, partly covered. Strain and allow to get cold.

Steep the lamb in the marinade for 24 hours in a refrigerator, turning twice if possible.

For the stuffing, cook the parsnips lightly in salted water, drain and dice. Fry the onion and garlic in oil or butter until soft and coloured. Mix with the cooked rice and chopped woodruff.

Drain the lamb on a rack for 1 hour and pat dry with a paper towel. Stuff the leg and tie into an even cylindrical shape.

Smear a little butter on the lamb and roast in a pre-heated oven at 400°F/200°C/Gas 6 for about 70 minutes, basting every 15 minutes and turning over after 40 minutes. Lift on to a clean dish, cover with foil and a couple of cloths, and leave to rest.

To make the gravy, tip off most of the fat from the roasting tin and brown the vegetables for a few minutes. Pour in the port to burn off the fat. Add the stock, lemon and cinnamon; season and simmer for 10 minutes. Strain into a saucepan, boil and skim off all fat. Reduce to a good consistency, add the redcurrant jelly and check for seasoning.

CHOCOLATE MOUSSE CAKE

Serves 8

8 oz (225g) best bitter dark chocolate
2 fl oz (50ml) coffee
6 eggs, separated
6 oz (175g) caster sugar
3 oz (75g) very soft unsalted butter

We use French 'Barrier' chocolate but Sainsbury's Luxury chocolate has a good cocoa fat content. The quality of the chocolate is critical. This is a simplified version of the recipe we use at the restaurant – as it partially contains uncooked eggs, make sure they are very fresh.

First melt the chocolate in the coffee.

Beat the egg whites until firm and add the sugar; beat until stiff. Mix the yolks with the warm chocolate, then divide the mixture into 2 parts and mix the butter into one half. Fold the meringue into both mixtures, then refrigerate the half containing butter.

Butter and sugar an 8 inch (20.5cm) cake tin and line the bottom with bakewell paper; turn the remaining half of the mixture into the tin. Bake at 350°F/180°C/Gas 4 for about 25 minutes until the centre is only just cooked – it should still wobble a little. Let it stand for 3 minutes, cover with a paper towel and turn out on to a rack to cool. Place on a serving plate and refrigerate. Ice the cake with the mousse which must also be well chilled.

An orange flavoured crème anglaise, sliced poached pears or a sorbet like blood orange make good accompaniments.

Sheila Kidd

THE ARK · ERPINGHAM

Everyone's dream idea – to own and run a restaurant? It is fun and great to earn a living doing something I enjoy so much – but what hard work! We thought when we arrived in the country, we would have an easier way of life but growing our own herbs and vegetables plus in the early days tending goats, hens and pigs and using their produce made for many aching limbs. Economically it is probably a disaster to produce such fresh vegetables but from the job satisfaction point of view there is nothing better. The vine leaves to wrap around mushrooms, the elderflowers for sorbet, sauces and drinks, blackberries and sloes in the autumn for 'puds' and liqueurs all make sure life is never dull. Herbs are a particular love of mine and last year the basil was marvellous to complement the Marmande tomatoes.
Lobster, crabs and sea trout are all good in this area so the summer is a bonus time but we often 'get it wrong' and end up with a surplus to requirements. Perhaps the hardest thing to learn is what to purchase when, and how to cope with waste.

BUCKWHEAT CRÊPES WITH MUSHROOM AND SOUR CREAM FILLING

Serves 6 – 8

FOR THE CRÊPES

1½ oz (40g) butter
12fl oz (350ml) milk
1 teaspoon sugar
1 teaspoon salt
1½ oz (40g) buckwheat flour
2½ oz (65g) plain flour
2 large free range eggs
2 tablespoons sunflower oil
3–4 fl oz (75–125ml) lager
melted clarified butter for cooking

FOR THE FILLING

2 medium onions, finely chopped
2–3 oz (50–75g) butter
1 clove garlic, chopped
1½ lbs (700g) flat or field mushrooms, chopped
juice of 1 lemon
½ pint (275ml) sour cream
chopped parsley

extra sour cream, chopped parsley and sautéed sliced mushrooms, to serve

Place the butter, milk, sugar and salt in a pan and gently warm until the butter has melted. Meanwhile mix the two flours in a bowl. Make a well in the centre and gradually mix in the beaten eggs and oil. Beat in the milk until you have a smooth batter. Pour in the lager, mix and leave in a cool place for at least 2 hours.

When ready to cook, bring back to a warm room temperature. Brush a 6–7 inch (15–18cm) cast iron pan with melted clarified butter and leave on the heat until very hot. Stir the batter and pour in a small amount to thinly coat the pan. When set, turn over and very briefly cook the other side. Turn out on to a plate and continue until all the batter is used. It is essential to have the pan very hot all the time and to make very thin crêpes.

To make the filling, soften the onion in butter and add the garlic and chopped mushrooms. Cook for a few minutes to drive off any moisture. Add the lemon juice and bubble on a high heat for a moment. Cool slightly, then stir in the sour cream, parsley and seasoning.

Fill each crêpe by putting a spoonful of the mushroom mixture on one quarter, fold in half, then fold again to quarter size. Arrange on a buttered ovenproof plate, brush the tops with melted butter and crisp in a very hot oven. Serve with extra sour cream and parsley and garnish with sautéed slices of mushrooms.

SEA TROUT WITH SPINACH AND HERB STUFFING IN A GREEN COAT

Serves 6 – 8

1 sea trout, scaled (leave whole or cut into fillets)
1 lb (450g) spinach or Swiss chard
juice of 1 lemon
small bunch tarragon, parsley, chives, chervil
2 tablespoons breadcrumbs
seasoning
1 beaten egg
2 tablespoons vermouth
large cabbage leaves, chard or Chinese leaves
5 fl oz (150ml) fish stock

FOR THE TOMATO AND BASIL COULIS
3 shallots, finely chopped
2 cloves garlic, crushed
1 stick celery, finely chopped
1 tablespoon sunflower oil
1 oz (25g) butter
3 fl oz (75ml) fish stock
2 fl oz (50ml) sherry
1½ lbs (700g) ripe tomatoes,
skinned and chopped
1 tablespoon brown sugar
salt and pepper
20 basil leaves

To make the stuffing, blanch the spinach and refresh in cold water, drain well and chop finely. Mix with the lemon juice, herbs, breadcrumbs, seasoning, beaten egg and vermouth. Stuff the cavity of the whole fish or spread the stuffing on the individual fillets.

Blanch and refresh the chosen leaves and wrap them round the fish. Then wrap the whole fish in oiled foil, pouring over a little fish stock and vermouth before sealing loosely. Place on a baking tray and bake at 350°F/180°C/Gas 4 for 20 – 25 minutes, depending on size. Test that the fish is cooked and leave to rest for 10 – 15 minutes. (Individual fillets should be placed in a small non-stick pan with a little fish stock and brought just to the boil. Cover with foil and place in a cool oven 325°F/170°C/Gas 3 for about 10 minutes.)

To make the tomato coulis, soften the shallots, garlic and celery in the oil and butter, without colouring. Add the stock and sherry and bubble for a few minutes before adding the rest of the ingredients. Simmer uncovered until reduced, then pass through a sieve.

To serve, pour a pool of tomato coulis on to individual plates and place the fish on top.

BAKED STUFFED PEACHES WITH AMARETTO FLAVOURED SABAYON

Serves 6

1 peach per person
mixture of Madeira cake crumbs,
chopped almonds and pine nuts
white wine
sugar

FOR THE SABAYON

3 egg yolks
2 whole eggs
2 tablespoons caster sugar
5 tablespoons Marsala or sherry
2 tablespoons Amaretto liqueur

Halve and stone the peaches and place in a buttered dish; fill the cavities with the nut mixture, pour some wine around the peaches, sprinkle with sugar and bake in a hot oven for 12–15 minutes.

To make the sabayon, place the eggs and yolks in a large basin over a pan of hot water. Add the sugar and whisk continuously until the mixture starts to thicken and froth. Whisk in the Marsala and sherry, then add the Amaretto. Continue until you have a thick foam and serve with the peaches. If making the sabayon in advance to serve cool, remove from the heat and whisk until cold.

Sonya Kidney

THE MARSH GOOSE · MORETON

When thinking about ideas for new dishes, I always look first of all at ingredients that are readily available, as I do not believe that the more you spend, the better the dish; imaginative use of what you have is most important. You should make good use of seasonal ingredients such as English asparagus and strawberries, incomparable in taste and not available all year. Also wherever your restaurant is located, trade should be tailored around locals, because you rely on them to fill your restaurant.

It may sound rather unhealthy, but the uncertainties, the stress, and sometimes the total chaos are some of the factors that I like about the restaurant trade. The best thing is the team spirit, when, for example, we all gather round as a new dish is being finished, tasting it, smelling it, making remarks as to how it could be improved. Of course there are also the staff shortages, the awkward customers, the long hours etc. but all of these are far outweighed by the pleasure you get from knowing that you are actually enjoying what you are doing.

STRAW POTATO CAKES FILLED WITH SMOKED COD AND LEEKS

Serves 4

2 large potatoes
oil
butter
seasoning
6 oz (175g) smoked cod
½ pint (275ml) milk
little double cream
1 leek, cut into fine strips, blanched and refreshed
chopped parsley

Grate the potatoes and season. Heat some oil and butter in a frying pan. Shape the potato into small, round cakes and fry on both sides until brown. Reduce the heat and cook the cakes through.

Poach the cod in a little milk seasoned with salt and pepper. Lift out the fish and reduce the milk until quite syrupy. Add the cream and leeks and warm well.

To assemble the dish, place one potato cake on the plate, with a little of the leek then some of the fish. Place a second potato cake on top, pour over a little of the sauce, sprinkle with chopped parsley and serve.

VEAL AND MUSHROOM HOLLANDAISE

Serves 4

8 oz (225g) unsalted butter
4 veal loin steaks, trimmed
oil
butter
salt and pepper
dash Madeira
½ pint (10 fl oz) veal stock

FOR THE HOLLANDAISE
little vinegar
few crushed peppercorns
chopped shallot
parsley stalk
3 egg yolks

FOR THE MUSHROOM DUXELLE
½ onion, finely chopped
12 oz (350g) mushrooms, finely chopped
little crushed garlic
1 oz (25g) butter
seasoning

Melt the 8 oz (225g) unsalted butter gently. Meanwhile, sweat the chopped onion and garlic in the 1 oz (25g) butter. When the onion is translucent, add the mushrooms and seasoning. Cook gently so that the liquid evaporates.

Place the vinegar, peppercorns, shallot and parsley in a small pan and heat until you have 1 tablespoon of liquid. Pour this on to the egg yolks and whisk together in a bowl over a pan of hot water until thick and hot. Ask someone to pour the melted butter into the bowl in a steady stream while you continue whisking. Do not use the solid butter which will have sunk to the bottom. Adjust the seasoning and keep the sauce warm.

Season the veal steaks and cook gently in a little oil and butter, turning over after 5 minutes – the meat should be cooked through. Remove the steaks and drain on kitchen paper.

Add a splash of Madeira to the pan and reduce. Add the veal stock and continue reducing until you have a gravy-like consistency.

Put 2 tablespoons of the Hollandaise and 1 tablespoon of the mushroom mixture in a bowl. Mix lightly and place on top of each veal steak. Brown under a hot grill until golden. Place in the centre of the plate and surround with the gravy. Serve with new potatoes and a tomato and lettuce salad.

WHITE AND DARK CHOCOLATE TERRINE

Serves 8

8 oz (225g) bitter chocolate
8 oz (225g) white chocolate
5 oz (150g) egg whites
10 oz (275g) caster sugar
3 fl oz (75ml) water
5 fl oz (150ml) sugar syrup,
made from 1 lb sugar and ½ pint water
dash rum
1 pint (570ml) cream
dash Grand Marnier

This terrine can be made well in advance. Melt each of the chocolates separately. Boil the caster sugar and water until the soft ball stage is reached (use a thermometer). As the sugar approaches the correct temperature, whisk the egg whites to a stiff foam. Pour on the boiling syrup and continue whisking until quite cold.

Fold the cold sugar syrup into the 2 chocolates and divide the mixture equally between 2 bowls. Lightly whip the cream and divide into two. Beat the dark chocolate into one half of the egg white mixture and when it is smooth add a dash of rum, followed by half the cream, mixing lightly but thoroughly. Follow the same procedure for the white chocolate, substituting Grand Marnier for the rum.

Line an oblong terrine with strong cling film and layer the 2 mixtures, starting and finishing with the dark chocolate. Fold the cling film over the top and freeze. Lift the terrine out and slice as required. Serve with a raspberry coulis.

Judy Knock

KINGSHEAD HOUSE · BIRDLIP

Recipes from the past tend to be viewed as comic curiosities and it is easy to make fun both of the vast quantities used and some of the bizarre instructions to the cook. Most of those which have survived in print are a reassurance that our predecessors in the kitchen were skilful, creative, and knew how to deal with their ingredients under far from perfect conditions. To attempt an 'authentic' dish from the past is a pointless and unrewarding task, for such great changes have taken place in the quality of the raw ingredients and in our ability to control cooking techniques that they cannot be recreated.

In our restaurant kitchen we attempt to find what those early cooks were looking for in terms of contrasts and combinations of flavours and texture in their dishes, and my menus borrow widely from earlier times. This may be as the occasional medieval dish appearing on our normal dinner menu, or in some of the special evenings we have here when food comes from one particular time or is the work of one famous chef of the past.

The dishes selected here are all based on 18th century recipes. This is a period which is particularly sympathetic to our own time. J. Austen-Leigh writing in 1870 commented 'Mistresses 100 years ago took a personal part in the higher branches of cooking', and in these pre-industrial times she would most probably have used the produce of her own farms and gardens. Food of this period was light in tone with liaisons of cream and eggs rather than with flour, and much use was made of fruit, vegetables and herbs. A wider variety of salad dressings were used in the 18th century than has ever been the case since.

MARINATED CHICKEN BREAST

Serves 6

3 large chicken breasts, off the bone
½ small onion, finely sliced
mixture of 3 or 4 fresh herbs (parsley, tarragon,
basil, chervil, fennel or dill) chopped
3 bay leaves
1 tablespoon English mustard
salt and pepper
juice of 1 lemon
5 fl oz (150ml) good oil (olive, walnut or sesame)
1 tablespoon white wine vinegar

Wrap the chicken breasts in foil and cook in a medium oven 350°F/180°C/Gas 4 for about 20 minutes until firm but not dried out. Remove the foil and keep the chicken juices.

Mix together the sliced onion and chopped herbs; put half this mixture in a container with the bay leaves. Lay the chicken breasts on top and then cover with the remaining mixture.

In a blender, mix together the mustard, salt, pepper, lemon juice, oil, vinegar and chicken juices. Pour this mixture over the chicken, cover and refrigerate for a minimum of 6 hours.

To serve, slice the chicken finely, pour over the marinade and serve with a salad of your choice.

LEG OF LAMB IN A MINTED CRUST

Serves 7 – 8

1 leg lamb, 4 – 5 lbs (1.8 – 2.3kg)
large bunch mint
1 oz (25g) butter
1 oz (25g) brown sugar
salt and pepper
1 tablespoon white wine vinegar
1 onion, chopped
1 carrot, chopped
1 stick celery, chopped
extra lamb bones
1 oz (25g) flour

Make small incisions in the meat and push in whole mint leaves. Then put the butter, sugar, seasoning, vinegar and all but a handful of the mint into a processor to make a paste and coat the lamb well with this.

Put the chopped vegetables into a baking tin with the lamb bones, cover with a sheet of foil and put the leg of lamb on top. Cook in a hot oven 425°F/220°C/Gas 7 for 20 minutes. Then turn the oven down to 350°F/180°C/Gas 4 and wrap the foil loosely round the lamb, so that it does not touch the crust. Return to the oven for 70 minutes or longer if you like well-done lamb, at 350°F/180°C/Gas 4.

Take the lamb out of the foil, carefully keeping the juices and put in a clean baking tin. Return to the oven, turned up to 400°F/200°C/Gas 6 for 20 minutes to crisp the outside while you make the sauce.

Discard the bones and place the remaining vegetables and fat in a pan. Stir in the flour and cook over a high heat, stirring all the time, for a couple of minutes. Add the meat juices left in the foil and let it cook for another couple of minutes, stirring the whole time. Liquidise, then sieve and adjust the seasoning, diluting the sauce if it is too thick. At the last moment add the remaining handful of chopped mint.

GOOSEBERRY AND ELDERFLOWER TART

Serves 8

*shortcrust pastry flan case 10 inches (25cm) wide
and 2 inches (5cm) deep, baked blind
2 lbs (900g) gooseberries
1 spray elderflowers, or use elderflower cordial
8 oz (225g) sugar
5 eggs
5 fl oz (150ml) cream
whipped cream, to serve*

Wash the gooseberries and put them in a saucepan with the elderflower spray if used and enough water to cover a third of the fruit. Cook until soft, stirring from time to time. Put in a blender, then push through a wire sieve. If you are using the cordial, add it at this point. This should yield approximately 1 pint (570ml) of gooseberry purée.

Whisk together the eggs and sugar until they are pale, fluffy and firm, add the cream and stir in the fruit purée. Pour this mixture into the flan case and bake at 350°F/180°C/Gas 4 for about 45 minutes. The flan is very light and will not bake very firm.

As it cools, sprinkle with icing sugar. Serve with whipped cream.

Lorna Levis

The kitchen 'At the Sign of the Angel' is not high tech but a hard-working domestic kitchen which revolves around our Aga. The relaxed atmosphere in the kitchen is carried through into our dining room by our staff who all live in the village and enjoy the extended family at the Angel.

Everything we use comes from as close to home as possible. First we raid the garden; for herbs – sorrel, fennel, parsley, thyme, sage, tarragon, mint, lovage and many others; vegetables, fruit, and our own ducks and hens. The net is then spread to the rest of the village; allotments, the 'big house' garden and a friendly market gardener. This takes care of nearly all vegetables and English fruit. The balance is from a wholesale supplier in Bath.

All our red meat comes from a single supplier with whom we have dealt for many years. He buys animals in local markets and all are butchered with the minimum of travelling and stress and the maximum humanity. Poultry also comes from local farms and game in season from local shoots.

Our salmon and trout are rod-caught and very fresh. Sea fish come from the fish market at Newlyn in Cornwall and are delivered overnight for use the next day.

SORREL SOUP

Serves 6

1 medium onion, peeled and finely chopped
2 oz (50g) butter
2 oz (50g) flour
1 small colander freshly picked and washed sorrel
3 pints (1.75 litres) turkey or chicken stock
½ pint (275ml) double cream
juice of half a lemon
salt and pepper
nutmeg

Fry the onion in the butter until soft but not brown. Add the flour to make a roux and cook gently. Liquidise the sorrel in the stock and add to the onion mixture. *Just* bring to the boil. Liquidise thoroughly. Add the cream and lemon juice, and season with salt, pepper and nutmeg. Reheat and serve.

ROAST DUCK WITH SAGE AND APRICOT STUFFING

Serves 4

1 lb (450g) onions, peeled and chopped
8 oz (225g) white breadcrumbs
1 oz (25g) fresh sage leaves, finely chopped
1 oz (25g) cashew nuts
2 oz (50g) dried apricots, coarsely chopped
salt and freshly milled black pepper
2 oz (50g) dripping
1 fresh duck, 5½ – 6 lbs (2.5 – 2.75kg)
with giblets
2 tablespoons flour
a little grated orange zest

FOR THE GRAVY

duck giblets
1 carrot
1 medium onion

Place the onions in a mixing bowl with the breadcrumbs, sage, cashew nuts, apricots, salt, pepper and melted dripping. Mix well. Pack the stuffing into the duck. Rub well with salt and flour, place on a grid in a dry roasting tin and roast in a hot oven for 1½ hours. Meanwhile, boil the giblets with the onion and carrot in 1 pint (570ml) water.

When the duck is cooked, remove from the tin and keep warm on a warmed serving dish. Pour off the surplus fat from the roasting tin, then over a gentle heat, stir 2 tablespoons flour into the duck juices. Add the orange zest and allow the mixture to brown. Gradually stir in the strained stock to make a rich gravy.

GOOSEBERRY AND ELDERFLOWER SORBET

Serves 4 – 6

2 lbs (900g) gooseberries
handful fresh elderflowers
8 oz (225g) granulated sugar
½ pint (225ml) water
½ pint (225ml) milk
½ beaten egg white

Boil the gooseberries, elderflowers and sugar in the water until the fruit is soft. Strain through a fine sieve. Stir in the milk and the egg white, mix well and freeze. An ice-cream maker produces much better results than simple freezing. Stir from time to time if using a freezer. If you have any elderflower wine available, stir in a cupful with the milk.

Eluned Lloyd and Judith Cooper

CNAPAN · NEWPORT

We are a mother and daughter team working together in the kitchen of Cnapan, which is a fine listed house in Newport. We have taken great care to create a homely atmosphere and take the same care when choosing our menu; we have wonderful fresh local produce which we transform into delicious meals, many of them traditional Welsh dishes like the ones chosen here. Our vegetables come from Chris Challoner (or Chris 'Organic') who lives in the Pwllheli hills and from Jeanette and Michael Wardle who also provide us with strawberries. Ben Levis supplies salmon from the River Teifi and Keith Bell lobsters and crabs from Cardigan Bay.

ANGLESEY EGGS

Serves 4

8 eggs
1½ lbs (700g) potatoes
6 leeks
knob of butter

FOR THE SAUCE

1 oz (25g) butter
1 oz (25g) plain flour
½ pint (275ml) milk
3 oz (75g) grated Cheddar cheese

Hard-boil the eggs, shell them and keep in cold water. Boil the potatoes, strain and mash them. Clean the leeks, cut into rings and cook in salted water for 10 minutes. Drain the leeks, add them to the potato with the butter and beat well.

Make a cheese sauce by melting the 1 oz (25g) butter; add the flour, season and mix well. Add the milk and 2½ oz (65g) of the cheese. Stir with a whisk until the sauce thickens and cook for 3 minutes.

Fork the leek and potato mixture around an ovenproof dish. Cut the eggs in half and arrange them in the centre. Pour over the cheese sauce and sprinkle with the remaining cheese. Place in a hot oven 400°F/200°C/Gas 6 for 20 minutes until golden brown.

PASTAI PEN Y BONT

Serves 4 – 6

FOR THE SAUCE

2 tablespoons olive or sunflower oil
1 medium onion, chopped
2 cloves garlic, crushed
3 teaspoons fresh root ginger, grated
2 tablespoons flour
½ pint (275ml) milk
1 tablespoon stem ginger, chopped
1 dessertspoon stiff yoghurt

FOR THE WHEAT LAYER

1 tablespoon olive oil
1 – 2 sticks celery, chopped
4 oz (125g) Bulghur wheat,
soaked in boiling water for 10 minutes
¼ teaspoon grated nutmeg
2 oz (50g) large, juicy raisins

FOR THE SPINACH AND NETTLE LAYER

1 oz (25g) butter
4 oz (125g) spinach, chopped
4 oz (125g) young nettle tops
(or the same quantity again of spinach)
grated zest and juice of 1 orange

4 oz (125g) Pencareg cheese (or Brie), sliced
2 oz (50g) Llanboidy cheese
(or Farmhouse Cheddar), grated

roughly buttered breadcrumbs with a
pinch of basil, fried off slightly

To make the sauce, heat the oil in a saucepan and cook the onion, garlic and ginger gently until soft. Stir in the flour and cook till it bubbles. Add the milk and bring the sauce to the boil, stirring as it thickens. Add the stem ginger and yoghurt.

To make the wheat layer, heat the olive oil in a pan and cook the celery. Add the fluffed up bulghur wheat, nutmeg, raisins and seasoning.

To make the spinach layer, melt the butter, add the spinach and nettles and cook until they wilt. Add the orange juice and zest.

Spread half the sauce over the bottom of a large ovenproof dish and cover with half the bulghur wheat. Cover this with half the spinach mixture, then the sliced Pencareg placed right across the dish. Spread the remaining bulghur over the cheese, top with the rest of the spinach and press down.

Cover the pie with the rest of the sauce and grate the Llanboidy cheese over the top. Scatter the crumbs over the pie and bake for 30 – 40 minutes at 375°F/190°C/Gas 5 until bubbling and crispy brown on top.

GINGERBREAD PUDDING

Serves 4 – 6

8 oz (225g) plain flour
pinch salt
4 oz (125g) brown sugar
4 oz (125g) margarine
½ teaspoon bicarbonate of soda
1 egg
4 oz (125g) golden syrup
5 oz (150g) black treacle
1 level teaspoon ginger
1 level teaspoon mixed spice
2½ fl oz (65ml) milk

Sift the dry ingredients. Melt the margarine, treacles and sugar and cool. Beat the egg with the milk. Add the treacle mixture and the egg mixture to the dry ingredients. Pour into a greased tin or dish about 10 x 10 inches (25 x 25cm) – the mixture will be sloppy.

Cook for approximately ¾ – 1 hour, depending on the oven, at 325°F/170°C/Gas 3. Serve with a sharp lemon sauce, good old custard or golden syrup.

Ann Long

Good cooking is often thought to be the exclusive province of trained chefs, but this is not so. I at least, did not begin as a potential chef, in fact my school report for Domestic Science remarked succinctly "conspicuously absent throughout the course"! I now spend almost every minute of every working day in the kitchen, because I cook for a living. I enjoy developing my skills and preparing food which not only looks good but tastes right. I feel a keen sense of pleasure in seeing my sweet or savoury sauces develop a lovely sheen, or in un-moulding a mousse that smells fragrant and perhaps hides a surprise flavour in its centre. I stress the importance of using fresh ingredients, carefully selected and presenting the finished dishes uncluttered, beautiful and clean-looking. When you give a dinner party you are really inviting your friends to share your delight in cooking and preparing a meal. Your guests are coming to see you and you want them to go home feeling happy; you will have taken care beforehand and during the cooking and serving and you should feel happy too.

SCALLOPS AND COURGETTES WITH BASIL MAYONNAISE

Serves 8

1 lb (450g) scallops, with corals
3 tablespoons hazelnut oil
1 tablespoon brandy
6 fl oz (175ml) lemon juice
1 teaspoon grated ginger
1 lb (450g) small firm courgettes

FOR THE CORAL CREAM

3 oz (75g) corals from the scallops
2 fl oz (50ml) single cream
Tabasco
salt and pepper

3½ fl oz (100ml) double cream
1 egg white
1 tablespoon chopped coriander
1 level tablespoon aspic
dissolved in 4 fl oz (125ml) boiling water

FOR THE BASIL MAYONNAISE

1 tablespoon lemon juice
1 teaspoon sea salt
4 tablespoons mayonnaise
4 tablespoons yogurt
2 oz (50g) chopped basil leaves

Cut the corals away from the white muscle and prick them with a needle to stop them bursting while cooking. Carefully remove the thin white skin around the scallops and cut each scallop into three downwards, with the grain.

Heat the hazelnut oil in a large frying pan,

add the sliced scallops and cook for a few seconds, shaking the pan. When they turn white, quickly tip them into a dish. Mix the lemon juice with the grated ginger and pour over the scallops.

Return the pan to the heat, add the corals and cook on each side until browned lightly. Reduce the heat, pour in the brandy and set it alight; allow the flames to die out. Transfer the cooked corals with any liquid to a small bowl and put to one side for the coral cream.

Cut a thin slice away from both ends of each courgette. Pass them through a shredder fitted with a medium disc. Spoon the courgette shoestrings into a sieve set over a bowl to drain. Remove the scallops from their marinade, lay the pieces on a towel and gently pat them dry. Using a sharp pointed knife cut each scallop down into thin strips.

Tip the courgettes into a small bowl. Using your hands, squeeze out all the juices and when you think you have finished, squeeze again. Transfer the dry shoestring courgettes to a mixing bowl.

Using your fingers, mix the courgettes and scallops together. Taste, twist in black pepper and taste again. With a pastry brush coat the inside of 8 x 6 fl oz (175ml) moulds or ramekins with a light vegetable oil.

Spoon the scallops and courgettes into ramekins. Using the back of your fingertips press the mixture firmly and evenly into the moulds and drain away any excess liquid. Transfer the dishes to a tray and put them in the refrigerator while you make the cream.

Place the corals in the food processor. Work until you have a smooth paste. Now add single cream. Mix together and add the seasoning. Pour the double cream into a mixing bowl and whisk until you have soft, almost floppy peaks. In another mixing bowl, whisk the egg white until light and fluffy.

Count 2 tablespoons of liquid aspic into the corals and mix until completely smooth and straight away pass it through a sieve on to the cream. With a metal spoon, fold the coral mixture into the cream then, still using a metal spoon, gently mix in the fluffy egg white and

chopped coriander. Gently spoon the cream on to the scallops and courgettes and using a pliable spatula, smooth the surface level. Return the filled moulds to the refrigerator.

To make the basil mayonnaise, put the lemon juice in a mixing bowl and add the sea salt. Stir with a wooden spoon until the salt has dissolved and gradually add the mayonnaise, yogurt and basil. Taste, twist in black pepper and taste again. Keep the flavoured mayonnaise in a container that has a lid.

To serve, run a thin knife around each scallop cream. Place the mould in one hand and cover it with the other. Invert the mould and shake it until you feel the cream fall into your hand. Let it drop back into the mould, then quickly turn it out on to a plate. Spoon the mayonnaise to one side of each scallop cream, garnish with coriander leaves and serve.

RABBIT FILLETS ON A BED OF ONION JAM IN A CRISP BREAD BOX WITH GAME SAUCE

Serves 8

8 rabbit saddles
hazelnut oil
butter
sprig rosemary

FOR THE SAUCE

2 oz (50g) butter
4 tablespoons flour
2 pints (1.1 litres) rabbit stock
1 tablespoon dried English mustard
1 tablespoon balsamic vinegar
1 teaspoon brown sugar
salt and pepper

FOR THE BREAD BOXES

1 white tin loaf, 2 – 3 days old
8 oz (225g) butter

2 lbs (900g) onions
3½ oz (100g) butter
1 tablespoon olive oil
6 oz (175g) caster sugar
2 teaspoons salt
8 tablespoons raspberry vinegar
½ pint (275ml) red wine
6 sage leaves, chopped
black pepper

Lay one rabbit, meat side up, on a board. Feel for the backbone and using a sharp pointed knife cut through the flesh to one side of the backbone and cutting against the ribcage, slice off the fillet. Repeat the same process with the other fillets.

To remove the membrane from each long wedge shaped fillet, lay the fillet flesh side up on the board, grip the thin end of the membrane, hold the knife at an angle and using a sawing action detach it from the meat. Rub the fillets with melted butter. In a large frying pan slowly heat a little oil with rosemary, add the fillets four at a time. Lightly seal them and using a spatula and your fingertips transfer them to a plastic or stainless steel tray. Form each warm fillet into a crescent and leave to cool.

To make the sauce, melt the butter in a heavy based saucepan over a low heat. Using a wooden spoon, stir in the flour and cook for 1 minute, stirring all the time. Raise the heat and gradually add the stock, blending until it boils and is smooth. Reduce the heat and simmer for 15 – 20 minutes, stirring often to prevent the sauce from sticking to the bottom of the pan.

Mix the mustard, vinegar and sugar together until smooth. Take the pan from the heat, taste, add the mustard mixture, twists of pepper and salt, gently stir these flavourings into the sauce and taste again. Pour into a plastic jug and keep covered with cling film.

For the bread boxes, set the oven to 325°F/170°C/Gas 3. Slice away the crusts of the bread and cut into 8 × 3 inch square shapes. Cut a square ¼–½ inch inside the bread shape, down to within ¼ to ½ inch from the base and slice the knife to one cut side, draw the blade out, then replace it with the blade facing the opposite way and slide it towards the other cut side to release the centre and carefully lift it out.

Slowly melt about 8 oz (225g) butter in a small saucepan. Using a pastry brush, coat the boxes one at a time with butter and set them standing upright on a cake rack resting on top of the shallow baking tray.

Bake them for about an hour, turning at regular intervals to allow the boxes to crisp and colour evenly. Leave on the cake rack to cool. Store in a kitchen paper lined, airtight tin. Rest them on a cake rack to heat through in the oven for a few minutes just before serving.

To make the onion jam, trim and peel the onions, remove the first fleshy layer and cut them in half vertically. Lay the halves cut side down on a board and cut them across into thin half moon slices.

Melt the butter and oil in a large saucepan and when it is hot tip in the onion, sugar and salt. Stir until glossy, cover with greaseproof paper and top with a tight fitting lid. Lower the heat as far as possible. Cook for about ¾ hour until tender. Uncover, draw the pan aside and mix in the vinegar, wine and chopped sage.

Return to a low heat and gently cook for about 30 minutes stirring often until the liquid has reduced to form a lovely syrupy glaze. Taste, twist in black pepper and taste again. Spoon the jam into a container that has a lid and leave to cool. Put a sheet of cling-film over the surface of the cooled onions, secure the lid and refrigerate.

Cut 8 x 10 inch (25cm) squares of double foil. Divide and spread the onion jam on each square and place 2 shaped fillets on top. Bring the sides of foil together and pleat over at the top to enclose the rabbit.

Set oven to 425°F/220°C/Gas 7. Cook the parcels on a hot tray near the top of the oven for 10 – 15 minutes.

Take out the rabbit parcels, carefully unseal each at the top, the fillets will be firm but springy to the touch. Leave to rest while you reheat the sauce and boxes. Spoon onion jam into each box and arrange 2 fillets on top. Ladle the sauce to cover half of the base of each plate. Slide a spatula under each filled box and lift it carefully to rest on the sauce. Serve them accompanied with broccoli garnished with crunchy toasted almonds and a dish of hot, crisp carrots.

STRAWBERRIES WITH CREAM CHEESE AND SHORTBREAD FINGERS

Serves 8

½ pint (275ml) red wine
1 stick cinnamon
1 teaspoon grated orange rind
3 oz (75g) caster sugar
1 tablespoon redcurrant jelly
2 lbs (900g) small strawberries

FOR THE SHORTBREAD

12 oz (350g) flour
8 oz (225g) soft butter
4½ oz (140g) caster sugar

FOR THE CREAM CHEESE

8 oz (225g) cream cheese
flavouring (e.g. nutmeg and lemon rind or cinnamon and orange rind)
5 fl oz (150ml) sugar syrup
½ pint (275ml) double cream

Pour the wine into a saucepan and add the cinnamon, orange rind, caster sugar and redcurrant jelly. Bring to the boil gently, stirring until the sugar and jelly have dissolved. Remove from the heat, leave to cool for 10 minutes and strain into a jug.

To make the shortbread, tip the flour into a large mixing bowl, cut the butter into small pieces and add it with the sugar to the flour. Work the ingredients to a dough with your fingertips. Cover with clingfilm and chill for 1 hour. Set the oven to 350°F/180°C/Gas 4. Press the shortbread into a lightly greased tin 8 x 12 inches (20.5 x 30.5cm) to a thickness of ½ inch (1 cm). Prick all over with a fork. Bake for 30–40 minutes until light and golden. Allow to cool then cut into 20 long fingers. Cool on a wire rack and store in an airtight tin when cold.

Beat the cream cheese until smooth and add the flavouring and sugar syrup. Gradually pour in the double cream and whisk until you have the thickness you like. Serve the chilled strawberries in a plain glass bowl and pour the wine over them at the table. Serve with the cream cheese and shortbread fingers.

Claire Macdonald

Kinloch Lodge, set on the shores of a sea loch on the Isle of Skye is very much our home, as well as the hotel we have been running for seventeen years. Supplies have vastly improved since the early days and we now have two local organic growers, though they, like everyone else are subject to the whims of the elements here. Everything possible is homemade, including the marmalade which we make in January for our guests' breakfasts throughout the year. We don't regard ourselves as professionals – we are still learning and enjoying ourselves in the process.

TOASTED GOATS CHEESE WITH WALNUTS AND LEEKS

Serves 4

6 medium sized leeks, well washed and trimmed, then sliced diagonally in bits about 1 inch (2.5cm)
2 oz (50g) walnuts
8 oz (225g) goats cheese (I use the log type)
4 slices of bread, cut into 1 inch (2.5cm) thickness

FOR THE VINAIGRETTE

½ teaspoon salt
good grinding black pepper
pinch caster sugar
1 tablespoon white wine vinegar
3 tablespoons walnut oil

I used to hate goats cheese until a few years ago when I tasted some and discovered just how delicious it is when hot. I think the flavour has a very great affinity with walnuts and leeks, and this salad of leeks vinaigrette with toasted walnuts makes the perfect accompaniment to the toasted goats cheese croûtons.

Mix together all the ingredients for the vinaigrette, mixing well. Steam the leeks until tender. Meanwhile toast the walnuts by shaking them over heat in a dry saucepan – I find this much easier than toasting them under a grill. Mix together the walnuts and leeks while the leeks are still hot and mix in the vinaigrette.

Toast the bread on both sides and slice off the crusts. Slice the rind off the cheese and divide it between the 4 slices of bread, spreading as evenly as possible. Toast under a hot grill until the cheese begins to melt – about 30 seconds. Serve immediately with the leeks and walnuts vinaigrette.

OSSO BUCO

Serves 6

4 tablespoons extra virgin olive oil
6 pieces shin veal,
each about 1½ – 2 inches (3.5 – 5cm) thick
2 onions, skinned and thinly sliced
1 tablespoon flour
1 tablespoon tomato purée
2 x 15 oz (425g) tins tomatoes
2 cloves garlic, skinned and finely chopped
¾ pint (400ml) dry white wine
salt
freshly ground black pepper
½ teaspoon sugar
grated zest of 1 lemon

Where I live, in the Isle of Skye, it is impossible to get veal shin for Osso Buco (impossible to get veal anything for that matter). As this dish is a particular favourite of mine, I make a point of buying the meat whenever I am away, to bring home and make into this most delicious of casseroles which freezes beautifully.

In a large, heavy casserole dish, heat the oil and brown the meat on both sides. Remove the pieces of veal from the dish and keep warm while you cook the sliced onions in the olive oil till they are soft and transparent looking (about 5 minutes). Stir in the flour and cook for a couple of minutes, then stir in the tomato purée.

Liquidise the contents of the tins of tomatoes and stir them into the onions and flour; add the garlic and wine. Stir until the sauce boils, then add salt, black pepper, sugar and lemon zest. Replace the veal pieces in the dish, pushing them down into the sauce. Cover the dish with a lid and cook in a moderate oven 350°F/180°C/ Gas 4 for 2 hours.

As with all casseroles, this one is best made, then cooled and reheated before serving. To reheat, take the casserole out of the fridge an hour before you put it into a moderate oven for a further 40 – 45 minutes cooking. The meat should be literally about to fall off the bone. One of the delights of this dish is the marrow in the middle of each piece of bone.

Serve with plain boiled Basmati rice into which you have stirred 2 tablespoons of finely chopped parsley, the finely grated rind of 1 lemon and 1 peeled clove of garlic, very finely chopped.

COFFEE AND ALMOND MERINGUE WITH CHOCOLATE SAUCE

Serves 6

3 egg whites
6 oz (175g) caster sugar,
flavoured with a vanilla pod
½ pint (275ml) double cream
2 teaspoons instant coffee
dissolved in 1 tablespoon boiling water
2 oz (50g) flaked almonds
icing sugar

FOR THE CHOCOLATE SAUCE

6 oz (175g) granulated sugar
3 rounded tablespoons cocoa powder
1 teaspoon vanilla essence
3 tablespoons golden syrup
(dip the spoon in very hot water first)
7 fl oz (200ml) boiling water

I have a particularly sweet tooth, as anyone who visits us at Kinloch will gather when they see the puds on our menu. I do love a sauce to accompany puds and this meringue cake with its coffee flavoured whipped cream filling and its scattering of toasted flaked almonds isn't quite complete for me without an accompanying chocolate sauce.

Line a baking tray with two circles about 6 – 8 inches (15 – 20cm) diameter of silicone parchment (non-stick greaseproof paper). In a bowl, whisk the egg whites till stiff, then, still whisking, gradually add the caster sugar a spoonful at a time, whisking till all the sugar is incorporated and the meringue is very stiff. Divide between the two marked circles and smooth evenly. Bake in a cool oven for about 2 hours or until you can lift each meringue half cleanly off the baking parchment. Cool. These meringues keep well in an airtight container. To fill, whip the cream, gradually adding the coffee. Sandwich together the meringue halves with the cream – at this stage you can freeze this meringue cake very successfully. Toast the flaked almonds and scatter them over the surface of the meringue with a dusting of sieved icing sugar.

Combine all the ingredients for the sauce in a saucepan and stir over a moderate heat till the sugar dissolves. Squash the cocoa against the sides of the pan with the back of a wooden spoon so that the sauce becomes smooth. Boil fast for 3 – 5 minutes – the longer you boil it the thicker the sauce becomes. Serve warm, with the meringue. Any leftover sauce can be stored in a screw-topped jar in the fridge.

Aileen Maguire

CRINGLETIE HOUSE HOTEL · PEEBLES

My husband and I were in our mid-forties when we fell in love with Cringletie and bought it. It was our first and only venture into the world of hotels and catering. With the enthusiasm of a complete novice I could hardly wait to get into the kitchen to take over the cooking. It was as I was sending up the first dishes in the hand operated dumb-waiter that the euphoria abated and I realised that we were now charging money for what had previously been my casual interest in cooking. Nearly twenty years on, we have dispensed with the dumb waiter but the 'butterflies' still persist!

CHEESE AND HERB GALETTE

Serves 8

FOR THE PANCAKES

4 oz (125g) plain flour
2 eggs
1 tablespoon oil
1 teaspoon salt
black pepper
8 fl oz (225ml) milk and water, mixed
melted butter
a little Parmesan cheese, grated

FOR THE FILLING

12 oz (350g) smooth cottage cheese
6 oz (175g) Cheddar cheese, grated
1 egg plus 1 egg yolk
3 tablespoons freshly chopped mint, parsley and chives, mixed
salt and black pepper to taste

Put all the pancake ingredients in a liquidiser or food processor and blend until smooth. Alternatively whisk all the ingredients together with a balloon whisk until smooth. Cover and allow to stand for 30 minutes.

Oil a 6 inch (15cm) omelette pan and cook the pancakes until golden on both sides. Layer with greaseproof paper and cover with a clean tea towel.

Blend all the filling ingredients together in a food processor until smooth or stir with a large fork until well mixed. Preheat the oven to 375°F/190°C/Gas 5. Butter the inside of a 6 inch (15cm) loose-bottomed cake tin and layer a pancake over the base, followed by a tablespoon of filling, smoothed over with the back of a spoon. Continue until everything is used up, finishing with a pancake. Brush with butter and sprinkle with Parmesan cheese. Cover with foil and bake for 35 minutes. Remove the foil and turn up the oven to 425°F/220°C/Gas 7. Bake for a further 5 minutes until golden brown.

Remove from the oven and allow to stand for 5 minutes before loosening the edges with a knife and removing from the tin to a warmed plate, Parmesan side uppermost. Serve in wedges garnished with salad.

CHICKEN SUPREME WITH MANGO, GINGER AND CORIANDER

Serves 6

6 chicken supremes, trimmed of all skin and fat
seasoned flour
oil and butter, for frying
2 tablespoons seasoned chicken stock,
or white wine
1 mango, peeled and chopped
2 oz (50g) butter
1 teaspoon fresh grated ginger
1 dessertspoon ground coriander
½ pint (275ml) double cream
salt and black pepper
fresh mint and parsley, to garnish

Coat the chicken in seasoned flour and fry lightly in a little oil and butter until golden. Transfer to a casserole dish. Pour round the stock or wine, cover and cook in the oven for 10 minutes at 350°F/180°C/Gas 4.

Meanwhile fry the chopped mango lightly in 2 oz (50g) butter, stirring in the spices after 1 minute. Cook for a further minute, then add the cream. Reduce slightly and season to taste with salt and black pepper.

Serve the chicken surrounded by the sauce and garnished with plenty of freshly chopped parsley or a sprig of fresh mint.

GLAYVA CRUNCH

Serves 8

4 oz (125g) toasted sifted oatmeal
4 oz (125g) toasted nibbed almonds
4 oz (125g) dark chocolate, grated
1 pint (570ml) double cream
1 oz (25g) caster sugar
¼ teaspoon vanilla essence
3 tablespoons Glayva
2 egg whites

Any other whisky liqueur could be substituted for the Glayva – of course you would then have to change the name of the dish!

Mix the oatmeal, almonds and chocolate together in a bowl, retaining a few almonds for decoration.

Whisk the cream with the sugar, vanilla essence and Glayva. Whisk the egg whites in a separate bowl and fold into the cream mixture. Fill a deep dish with alternate layers of the two mixtures, finishing with a sprinkling of the almonds.

Joyce Molyneux

The Carved Angel is lucky in its situation, being able to draw on a wide selection of fish; salmon out of the River Dart and lobster, crab and prawns caught locally. It enjoys the support of first class greengrocers and butchers, together with a local grower who grows unusual vegetables, herbs and fruit.

PIMENTO SOUFFLÉ SUISSESSE

Serves 4

1 pimento, diced
¼ pint (150ml) milk
1 oz (25g) butter
½ clove garlic
1 oz (25g) flour
seasoning
1 tablespoon Parmesan
chopped parsley
2 eggs, separated
¼ pint (150ml) double cream

Heat the milk with half the pimento and whizz in a blender. Melt the butter and sweat the remaining pimento with the garlic. Add the flour, seasoning and Parmesan and cook, stirring, for a few minutes.

Pour on the milk mixture and add the chopped parsley; beat well and cool slightly. Add the yolks and beat again. Whisk the egg whites and fold into the mixture. Divide between 4 buttered moulds and cook in a bain-marie for 20 minutes at 425°F/220°C/Gas 7.

Turn out when cool on to an ovenproof dish, pour over the cream, sprinkle with Parmesan and bake in a hot oven for 6 minutes. Serve immediately.

BRILL WITH A BASIL AND PINE KERNEL TOPPING

Serves 4

FOR THE CRUST
2 oz (50g) pine kernels, lightly roasted
fresh basil, chopped
olive oil
seasoning
2 oz (50g) soft crumbs

2 shallots, chopped
butter
4 x 5 oz (150g) brill fillets
white wine
2 tablespoons diced fresh tomato

Mix the roasted pine kernels in a food processor with the basil, oil and seasoning. Add to the crumbs in a bowl.

Sweat the shallots in a little butter in an ovenproof dish and place the brill fillets on top. Season and turn over, then spread the crust mixture evenly over the fish. Pour round a little white wine and add the diced tomato. Cook gently in the oven for 10 – 15 minutes at 275°F/140°C/Gas 1. Check the juice and brown under the grill before serving.

GRAPES IN MUSCAT JELLY

Serves 4

4 sheets gelatine, soaked in cold water
2 oz (50g) caster sugar
½ pint (275ml) water
½ pint (275ml) Muscat de Beaumes de Venise
juice of half a lemon
48 grapes, peeled and pipped
sweet cicely, to decorate

Heat the sugar and water until the sugar has dissolved. Add the gelatine and stir to dissolve completely. Add the Muscat and sharpen with the lemon juice, then cool. Layer the jelly with the grapes in 4 glasses. Decorate with a sprig of sweet cicely.

Alison Parsons and Barbara Drury

POLMAILY HOUSE · DRUMNADROCHIT

We have been at Polmaily House for eight years. The hotel faces south on the slopes of Glen Urquhart near the village of Drumnadrochit on the shores of Loch Ness. We base our menus on the best and freshest local ingredients – an Ullapool fisherman delivers langoustines; grouse comes from Sutherland; we get a good supply of fruit and vegetables from the Edinburgh markets and one Glasgow supplier even does a weekly run from the markets in Paris. We have Aberdeen Angus beef and the justly-famed Highland lamb. Guests are always surprised at the wide range of Scottish farm cheeses we offer and we are also proud of our extensive wine cellars.

ORKNEY SCALLOPS IN PUFF PASTRY SHELLS WITH WHITE PORT AND CREAM

Serves 4

16 scallops
½ pint (275ml) water
1 bay leaf
6 peppercorns
½ lb (225g) puff pastry
egg wash, for glaze
4 scallop shells (round half)
pepper
3 fl oz (75ml) white port
7 fl oz (200ml) double cream
juice of half a lemon
1 heaped tablespoon each julienne of carrot, celeriac, green part of leek, blanched and refreshed

Trim the muscle from the scallops. Place in a pan with the water, bay leaf and peppercorns. Bring to the boil and simmer for 30 minutes. Strain and reserve the liquid for making the sauce.

Roll the pastry to ¼ inch (0.5cm) thickness and use to line the 4 well scrubbed and greased scallop shells. Brush with egg wash and bake in a hot oven (425°F/220°C/Gas 7) for 12 – 15 minutes until well risen and golden. Make a slit to release the steam.

Meanwhile cut the coral from the scallops and slice the white meat into 2 or 3 thin circles; season with a little pepper. Heat a lightly oiled large frying pan, add the scallops and cook on one side only for 1 minute. Keep warm. Deglaze the pan with white port, fish stock and cream, reduce slightly until thickened and add the lemon juice and seasoning. Return the scallops to the pan with the julienne vegetables until heated through. Cut open the pastry shells leaving a hinge at the back and place one on each of 4 hot plates. Divide the scallops between the shells, pour over the remaining sauce and serve at once.

WILD MUSHROOM RAVIOLI WITH FRESH TOMATO SAUCE

Serves 4

FOR THE MUSHROOM DUXELLE

1 shallot, chopped
butter
3 oz (75g) chanterelles
3 oz (75g) ceps, or any other wild mushrooms
fresh marjoram
1 tablespoon crème fraîche

FOR THE PASTA

3 oz (75g) plain flour
2 large eggs
1 tablespoon milk
salt

FOR THE TOMATO SAUCE

2 shallots
1 clove garlic
butter
10 fresh tomatoes
fresh marjoram
½ pint (275ml) vegetable stock
salt and pepper
2 oz (50g) butter

To make the mushroom duxelle, sweat the shallot in butter until soft, then add the finely chopped mushrooms and marjoram. Cook for about 8 minutes, leave to cool, then blend with the crème fraîche.

Make the pasta in the usual way or buy fresh if you are feeling lazy, and put through a hand pasta machine a piece at a time, keeping the remainder moist-wrapped in clingfilm. Using a tiny round fluted cutter cut out circles of pasta. Place 1 teaspoon of the mushroom mixture on one pasta circle and cover with another, sealing the edges tightly with your fingers; continue until all the mixture is used up. Lay the prepared ravioli on a tea towel on a tray, leaving a space between each.

For the tomato sauce, sweat the shallots and garlic in butter, then add the roughly chopped tomatoes, marjoram, stock and salt and pepper. Cook for about 10 – 12 minutes, liquidise, then sieve. Return to the heat and stir in 2 oz (50g) butter. Check for seasoning.

Cook the ravioli in a very large pan of boiling water until they rise to the surface. Drain and serve with the tomato sauce.

PEACH ICE CREAM

Serves 4

4 egg yolks
½ pint (275ml) milk
10 oz (275g) sugar
10 fresh peaches, blanched,
skinned and poached in sugar syrup

FOR THE BRANDY BASKETS

4 oz (125g) butter
4 oz (125g) demerera sugar
4 oz (125g) golden syrup
4 oz (125g) plain flour
pinch salt
1 teaspoon ground ginger
1 teaspoon lemon juice
2 – 3 drops vanilla essence

raspberry coulis
and lightly whipped cream to serve

Make a crème anglaise with the egg yolks, milk and sugar.

Liquidise 6 of the peaches with 5 fl oz (150ml) sugar syrup and 2–3 cracked kernels. Cool and add to the cooked custard mixture. Freeze in an ice-cream machine. Halve and stone the remaining peaches and conserve in sugar syrup.

To make the brandy baskets, put the butter, sugar and syrup in a saucepan and heat gently until the butter has melted and the sugar dissolved. Leave to cool slightly. Sift the flour with the salt and ginger into the mixture. Stir well and add the lemon juice and vanilla essence.

Put teaspoons of the mixture on to a well greased baking sheet at least 4 inches (10cm) apart and cook for 8 minutes in a preheated oven at 325°F/170°C/Gas 3. Leave the biscuits for 2–3 minutes then remove them with a sharp knife and use small pudding bowls to shape into baskets.

To serve, place half a peach in the bottom of each basket, held in place by a thin layer of ice-cream on the dish. Top with a scoop of ice-cream and surround with a raspberry coulis feathered with lightly whipped cream.

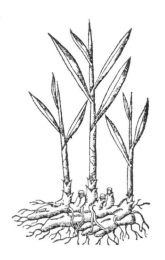

Jane and Elizabeth Pelly

THE MANOR HOUSE INN · CARTERWAY HEADS

We are lucky enough to have a marvellous supply of locally grown herbs and vegetables which we rely heavily upon. The chicken dish uses a lot of mint; and the vegetables come from the garden of Minstreacres Monastery which is run by the Passionist Fathers; the garden is looked after by many of our locals. We have a marvellous local butcher who kills all his own meat and therefore we know we can rely on the best beef for the satay which is one of the most popular first courses that we have – a lot of our customers seem to enjoy an oriental flavour! We currently change the restaurant menu once a month; but sometimes we find customers request us to retain old favourites – the Chicken Hymettus is one of these.

BEEF WITH SATAY SAUCE

Serves 4

12 oz (350g) rump steak, cubed

FOR THE MARINADE

2 fl oz (50ml) olive oil
1 level teaspoon chilli powder
1 tablespoon Worcester sauce
juice of 1 lemon
2 tablespoons chopped fresh mint

FOR THE SATAY SAUCE

1 medium onion, finely chopped
2 cloves garlic, minced
oil
1 teaspoon chilli powder, to taste
1 tablespoon creamed coconut
4 oz (125g) crunchy peanut butter
1 tablespoon mango chutney

We use cocktail sticks for starter size helpings and it's advisable to soak them in cold water before cooking, to prevent burning.

Soften the onion and garlic in a tablespoon of oil. Add the chilli powder and cook. Then add the coconut, peanut butter and chutney. Add approximately 4 fl oz (125ml) water and stir over heat until a creamy thick sauce is reached – you may need to add more water.

Thread 3 or 4 cubes of marinated meat on to skewers and grill or fry over a high heat for 3 – 4 minutes, turning once.

Arrange on a plate with a spoonful of warm satay sauce and, if liked, a spoonful of Greek yoghurt into which some chopped fresh mint has been stirred.

CHICKEN HYMETTUS

Serves 4

4 chicken breasts
finely grated zest and juice of 3 limes
good pinch saffron strands
1 oz (25g) butter
4 tablespoons sunflower oil
2 tablespoons clear honey
2 level teaspoons chopped fresh mint
salt and ground black pepper
1 oz (25g) flaked almonds

The name comes from Mount Hymettus in Greece, famous for its honey; the honey for this recipe does not necessarily have to be from Mount Hymettus!

Prick the chicken breasts and place in a shallow dish. Sprinkle with the grated zest and juice from the limes, cover the dish and marinate in the refrigerator for up to 3 days. Turn the chicken occasionally.

When ready to cook, soak the saffron strands in boiling water for 20 minutes, then strain, reserving the liquid.

Melt the butter and oil in a large, heavy based pan. Remove the chicken from the marinade and add to the pan; fry over a brisk heat until golden brown on all sides.

Mix the honey with the saffron liquid and the marinade, then pour over the chicken. Add the thyme, half the mint and salt and pepper. Cover the pan and simmer gently for 45 minutes until the chicken is tender, basting occasionally.

Toast the almonds under the grill and mix with the remaining mint – to serve, sprinkle this mixture over the chicken and its juices.

LEMON MERINGUE ICE CREAM

Serves 4

1 pint (570ml) whipping cream
8 oz (225g) carton Greek yoghurt
6 – 8 homemade meringues
½ pint (275ml) homemade lemon curd

Whip the cream and yoghurt together until fairly stiff. Crush the meringues and fold into the cream mixture. Stir in two-thirds of the lemon curd and freeze.

To serve, dribble a few teaspoons of the remaining lemon curd over a large scoop of the ice cream.

Carla Phillips

We started the restaurant in June 1986. A Regency building, just off the quay of a busy little port we knew well – in a comparable small French town this would undoubtedly be the location for the restaurant. We serve whatever is fresh and locally available: local fish, shellfish and game – constantly changing the menu to offer whatever has just arrived. However, customer insistence has ensured that certain dishes always remain on our menu – such as the Butterscotch Pie.

The menu I have chosen reflects the humbler ingredients which are frequently on offer. We do serve sea trout and sea bass, and each Sunday we roast a sizeable chunk of local venison. But squid from the North Sea and pigeon, universally available (and detested by farmers) can be stars of a meal as well!

SQUID SALAD

Serves 8 – 10

about 1 lb (450g) baby squid
2 tablespoons olive oil
3 – 4 large cloves garlic, crushed
1 dessertspoon Hungarian (mild) paprika
juice of 3 lemons
handful chopped parsley
freshly milled black pepper

If only larger, older squid is available, it may be casseroled for at least half an hour, rather than cooked rapidly. Otherwise this recipe will still apply.

Clean the squid by first separating the two parts of the body, removing the plastic-like quill and the ink sac. You can use all the firm flesh, which includes the tentacles as well as the main coat. Peel off all the darker, membrane-like skin you can (don't worry abut that covering the tentacles). Score the body lightly with a knife in criss-cross cuts, then slice it into bite-sized triangles. This Chinese technique makes the pieces curl up when cooked, looking decorative and somehow marine in appearance. Cut the tentacles into smallish pieces as well.

Heat the olive oil in a large, heavy-bottomed frying pan or casserole and when very hot, add the squid. Sauté it rapidly, turning it round. When it turns opaque, starting to exude juices, wait a second or two and add the garlic, followed by the paprika, stirring well to make sure the squid is evenly coated. Lastly add the lemon juice, parsley and pepper. Allow to cook for a couple of minutes, stirring, then taste a piece; it should be tender, not at all rubbery. Remove from the heat and allow to cool, then stir it round and chill well for a few hours. It should be served simply, spooned on to various salad greens and sprinkled with more parsley.

PIGEON BREASTS WITH PORT, WINE AND CREAM

Serves 6

knob butter
12 pigeon breasts (a pair per person)
few thin onion rings, cut up finely
salt
parsley
thyme
6 tablespoons port
6 tablespoons red wine
6 dessertspoons whipping or double cream

This is extremely quick to prepare, so that it is a good idea to organise the rest of the meal in advance. It's also an efficient method for using wood pigeon – gutting and plucking the bird is unnecessary. A sharp incision by the breastbone, and the meat of the breast can easily be carved out with a sharp little knife.

Heat a large, heavy-bottomed frying pan and melt a small knob of butter. Rapidly add the pigeon breasts. Brown them well on one side for about 2 minutes. Then turn, add the onion fragments and season with a little salt, pepper, chopped parsley and thyme. After about a minute, add the port. Allow it to heat, then either tilt the pan or light it with a match (standing well back), to allow the alcohol to burn off. When the flames have died down, add the red wine. When the liquid has started to reduce, looking slightly glassy, add the cream and allow the sauce to brown and thicken somewhat. Remove from the heat and finely slice the pigeon, either into small, fanlike fragments or tiny, thin fingers. Serve on toast or croûtons, covered with the sauce.

BUTTERSCOTCH PIE WITH A WALNUT CRUST

Serves 8

FOR THE CRUST

12 oz (350g) crushed walnuts
4 oz (125g) melted butter
1 oz (25g) caster sugar
pinch salt

FOR THE FILLING

4 oz (125g) salted butter
3 oz (75g) light brown sugar
3 oz (75g) dark brown sugar
1 teaspoon salt
3 teacups milk
1 cup whipping cream
3 level tablespoons cornflour
3 fl oz (75ml) boiling water
1 teaspoon vanilla essence

Mix together the ingredients for the crust and press into the bottom and sides of a lightly oiled large baking dish. Bake in a medium oven 350°F/180°C/Gas 4 for 15 minutes. Allow to cool while you prepare the filling.

Add the whipping cream to 2 teacups of the milk and heat together very gently. Mix the cornflour into the remaining cup of milk. Melt the butter with the salt (retaining a small knob of butter) until it starts to bubble, then rapidly add both the sugars. Stir well until it just starts to bubble again, then add the boiling water. Stir, but stand back, as it spits.

Now mix together the cornflour-milk mixture with the heated milk and cream mixture. Add these to the brown sugar-butter mixture. Stir over a medium heat until it thickens and starts to bubble. Remove from the heat, stirring well and add the vanilla and the remaining knob of butter. Pour the mixture into the baked crust. Chill well and serve with cream, decorated with a few walnuts.

Margaret Rees

Fresh local produce is used in all our dishes. The menu changes monthly with dishes being chosen either because they are traditional or new recipes which illustrate the demands of adventurous modern tastes in eating and new dietary habits. We are fortunately situated in the middle of a rich agricultural area which produces excellent fresh produce. Local farms supply us with unadulterated fresh cream, yogurts, free range eggs, interesting new soft and hard cheeses. Organically grown fruit and vegetables together with organically reared poultry and meat are used whenever possible. We use wholemeal flour ground by the local watermill.

The local anglers yield a rich supply of salmon, sewin and trout, while the fish markets of Swansea and Milford Haven are a good source of wet fish and shell fish. Cockles and laverbread from Penclawdd are a unique local delicacy. Welsh vineyards at Llanarth and Monow Valley provide interesting white wines. We grow in our own garden sixty different herbs, unusual vegetables and soft fruits. The local country hedgerows are alive with wild flowers, fruits and herbs which are preserved in jams, jellies and wines.

LAVERBREAD ROULADE

Serves 8

1 lb (450g) laverbread
4 eggs, separated
¼ teaspoon nutmeg
zest of ½ orange

FOR THE FILLING

8 oz (225g) low fat cream cheese
1 tablespoon orange juice
2 tablespoons chopped herbs
(mint, parsley, chives or tarragon)
1 tablespoon cream or yogurt

FOR THE TOMATO COULIS

8 tomatoes

Mix together the laverbread, egg yolks, nutmeg and orange zest. Whisk the egg whites until stiff and fold into the mixture. Pour into a lined Swiss roll tin and bake for 10–12 minutes in a moderate oven. Turn on to a sheet of parchment paper and roll up immediately. Leave until cold or freeze at this stage.

Mix all the ingredients for the filling together. Unroll the roulade and spread the filling over. Roll up firmly. Other flavourings may be added to the filling, such as ham, smoked salmon or prawns. Serve sliced as a starter or whole as a buffet dish.

To make the tomato coulis, blanch the tomatoes in boiling water and skin. Chop coarsely and liquidise. Pass through a sieve and serve with the roulade.

LAMB IN ELDERFLOWER CHAMPAGNE

Serves 6 – 8

FOR THE MARINADE

*1 onion, chopped
1 carrot, chopped
2 tablespoons oil
1 pint (570ml) elderflower champagne
(see below) or white wine
3 fl oz (75ml) vinegar
6 juniper berries
2 cloves garlic, chopped
1 sprig thyme
1 sprig rosemary
1 bay leaf
seasoning*

*1 boned leg or shoulder of lamb, firmly rolled,
about 5 lbs (2.3kg)
2 tomatoes*

FOR THE ELDERFLOWER CHAMPAGNE

*3 heads of elderflower
1 tablespoon white wine vinegar
8 pints (4.4 litres) water
1½ lbs (700g) sugar
juice of 1 lemon*

To make the champagne, combine all the ingredients in a sterelised container and leave to stand for 48 hours. Strain and pour into screw top bottles. Drink or use within 2 weeks.

Mix together all the ingredients for the marinade and pour over the meat. Leave to marinate for 2 days. Remove the meat from the marinade and strain the vegetables.

Brown the meat in a casserole, add the vegetables and sweat until lightly coloured. Add the liquid marinade, tomatoes and enough water to cover the joint. Cook in the oven for about 1½ hours at 350°F/180°C/Gas 4. Remove the bay leaf and the joint. Liquidise the vegetables and stock and strain. Simmer for 10 minutes and serve poured over the meat.

FRESH LIME CHEESECAKE WITH RASPBERRY COULIS

Serves 6 – 8

FOR THE BASE

*8 oz (225g) digestive biscuits
1 oz (25g) butter
1 tablespoon golden syrup
zest of 1 lime*

FOR THE FILLING

*4 oz (125g) cream cheese
2 oz (50g) icing sugar
juice of 2 limes
5 fl oz (150ml) cream
2 teaspoons gelatine
3 tablespoons water
2 egg whites*

FOR THE COULIS

*8 oz (225g) raspberries
2 oz (50g) caster sugar*

Crush the biscuits and add the melted butter and syrup. Press into the base of an 8 inch (20.5cm) dish and sprinkle with lime zest, reserving some for the top.

Place the cream cheese, sugar, juice and cream in a bowl and mix well or use a food processor. Melt the gelatine in the water and cool. Whisk the egg whites. Pour the gelatine into the mixture and fold in the egg whites. Pour over the biscuit base and sprinkle with remaining lime zest. Leave to set for 1 hour.

To make the coulis, liquidise the raspberries with the sugar and pass through a sieve. Serve the sauce with the cheesecake.

Nerys Roberts

Y BISTRO · LLANBERIS

We are lucky in being able to adapt a wide range of local produce — char from a nearby lake, Welsh lamb, soft fruits, Welsh cheeses, local meat, fish and game — for traditional recipes; we won the Taste of Wales award in 1986. We alter the menu six times a year to follow seasonal changes, with six items on each course. We have been here for eleven years and our regular customers always let us know which dishes they want to remain on the menu!

FRESH GINGER AND LETTUCE SOUP

Serves 4

2 onions, finely chopped
2 carrots, finely chopped
1 iceberg lettuce, shredded
4 slices root ginger, peeled
parsley stalks
flour
1¾ pints (1 litre) good homemade chicken stock
cream to finish
croûtons and chopped parsley to garnish

Sauté the onions and carrots until soft but not coloured. Turn the heat up and quickly sauté the lettuce, ginger and parsley stalks until they wilt, then add flour to make a roux. Work for a few minutes then add the hot chicken stock. Simmer for 5 minutes (no more or the lettuce will turn brown). Liquidise and sieve into a clean pan. Stir in the cream and serve with croûtons.

BEST END OF LAMB WITH ALMOND AND PARSLEY SAUCE

Serves 4

2 best ends of Welsh lamb, each with 6 cutlets
juice of 1 lemon
1 tablespoon chopped parsley
1 tablespoon chopped almonds
1 tablespoon chopped fresh rosemary
butter
2 garlic cloves, crushed

FOR THE SAUCE

3 egg yolks
1 tablespoon chopped parsley
1 tablespoon chopped almonds
rind of 1 lemon
salt and pepper
1 clove garlic
6 oz (175g) unsalted butter

Ask the butcher to chine the meat, cut the bones down to a reasonable size and scrape the ends clean. Remove the skin, score the fat with a sharp knife and cut each best end in half to make 4 portions of 3 cutlets each.

Mix all the other ingredients to form a paste, spread over the meat and leave for a couple of hours. Cook for 15 minutes at 425°F/220°C/Gas 7 then reduce to 375°F/190°C/Gas 5 for 15 – 30 minutes depending on taste.

To make the sauce, blend the egg yolks with all the other ingredients except the butter. Heat the butter until foaming and pour on to the yolk mixture in a slow steady stream, whisking constantly until the sauce is thick and creamy; the sauce must be served immediately – it will not reheat.

Serve the lamb with cutlet frills and the sauce separately. Local new potatoes, Cauliflower Polonaise and a crisp green salad go well.

SNOWDON PUDDING

Serves 4

4 oz (125g) raisins
6 oz (175g) beef suet
1½ oz (40g) ground rice
6 oz (175g) soft brown sugar
8 oz (225g) soft white breadcrumbs
6 oz (175g) lemon marmalade
2 lemons, grated
6 beaten eggs
pinch salt

FOR THE SAUCE

3 oz (75g) caster sugar
5 fl oz (150ml) water
zest and rind of 1 lemon
¾ pint (400ml) medium dry wine
1 teaspoon flour
2 oz (50g) butter

Well grease a large pudding dish or tin and sprinkle half the raisins on the bottom. Mix all the other ingredients together and bind with the egg. Pour the mixture into the prepared tin or dish, cover and steam for 2 hours.

To make the sauce, boil the sugar, lemon rind and water to make a syrup (about 10 minutes). Add the wine and simmer for 3 – 4 minutes. Beat the flour and butter together, whisk into the sauce, sieve and serve hot with the pudding which will freeze and reheat beautifully!

Ruth Roberts

We have been running Lynwood House as a restaurant, and more recently a 'restaurant with rooms' for twenty-one years. We have now expanded into a family business with one of our sons working alongside me in the kitchen and the others running the restaurant with their father. Seafood is our particular speciality and, in common with all the ingredients used, is fresh and locally produced. Mussels come from Fremington, wild salmon in season from the River Lyn, caught by rod and line, local Dovers, turbot, brill and bass. Loch Fyne provides us with smoked salmon and langoustines and we have game in season from local shoots. Vegetables are almost 100% organic from four small market gardens ranging from Exmoor to Bideford with cream and eggs from a local farm. Even our glassware is local – from Dartington!

SMOKED SALMON PÂTÉ

Serves 10

8 oz (225g) smoked salmon trimmings
8 oz (225g) peeled, cooked prawns
8 oz (225g) butter
juice of half a lemon
pinch cayenne pepper
5 fl oz (150ml) double cream
lemon wedges, toast and salad, to serve

Blend all the ingredients except the cream in a food processor until smooth. Place in a bowl and carefully fold in the cream. Place the mixture on to a piece of clingfilm and roll up into a sausage shape about 1½ inches (3.5 cm) in diameter. Chill in a refrigerator, then slice and serve with lemon wedges, hot toast and a little tossed salad of various leaves. The pâté can be made 2 – 3 days in advance.

POACHED BREAST OF PHEASANT WITH QUENELLES

Serves 10

5 pheasants
2 carrots
1 onion
2 sticks celery
1 sprig each fresh thyme, parsley, marjoram
1 bay leaf

FOR THE QUENELLES

boned thigh meat, chopped
for each 1 lb (450g) boned flesh:
4 oz (125g) egg whites, ½ teaspoon salt, juice of 1 lemon, 5 fl oz (150 ml) double cream

FOR THE SAUCE

1½ pints (900ml) stock
1 pint (570ml) red wine
15 fl oz (400ml) double cream
seasoning to taste
4 oz (125g) onion
4 oz (125g) carrot
4 oz (125g) celeriac
4 oz (125g) leeks
1 bunch radishes

Start preparations the day before. Skin the pheasants, remove the legs and cut in half (drumsticks and thighs). Take off the breasts and remove the wing bones. Cover the breast and keep in the refrigerator until needed.

First make the stock: put the carcasses, drumsticks, skin and other bones in a large pan with the vegetables and herbs. Bring to the boil, then simmer for 4–5 hours. Strain and cool.

To make the quenelles, take all the flesh off the thighs, removing any sinew. Blend in a food processor with the egg whites and salt until smooth. Add the lemon juice and lastly the cream. Chill for 24 hours in the refrigerator.

Finely slice the vegetables. Poach the pheasant breasts on top of the stove in the stock and red wine. Simmer lightly until almost cooked (about 5 minutes). Place on a baking tray, cover with tin foil and keep warm in a low oven. They will finish cooking while you make the sauce.

Use 2 dessertspoons to form the quenelle mixture into nut shapes. Poach them in red wine and stock for 2–3 minutes and put with the pheasant breasts to keep warm. Turn up the heat under the sauce, add the cream and reduce by half until the sauce coats the back of a wooden spoon. Add the finely sliced vegetables to the sauce with seasoning.

Serve each pheasant breast together with 2 or 3 quenelles, masked with the sauce and vegetables, which should still be crunchy, and plain boiled new potatoes in their skins.

CREME CARAMELS

Serves 10

FOR THE CARAMEL

1 gill water
10 dessertspoons granulated sugar

FOR THE EGG CUSTARD

4 large whole eggs
2 dessertspoons caster sugar
5 fl oz (150ml) milk
1¼ pints (700ml) double cream
clotted cream, to serve

Put 10 ramekin dishes in a roasting tin with cold water to come half way up the sides of the dishes. Put the sugar and water into a saucepan over a high heat and leave until the mixture is a golden colour. Pour a little into the bottom of each dish.

Liquidise the eggs, sugar, milk and cream to make 2 pints (1.1 litres) of mixture. Blend, then pour into the ramekin dishes. Place in the centre of the oven 275°F/140°C/Gas 1 for 2 hours. Test for setting before removing from the oven. Take out of the bain marie and cool overnight in the refrigerator.

Slide a knife around the dish and turn out on to a plate. Serve with Devonshire clotted cream.

Sylvia Rosen

LANGLEY WOOD · REDLYNCH

Situated as we are in the heart of the countryside, supplies at Langley Wood are drawn from a wide area and hunting out the best local produce is part of the fun of the business. Even the watercress is picked fresh from the beds some fifteen miles away. In the summer we often pick our own fresh produce from a local farm. The mushroom recipe was included because mushrooms are one of the few things delivered fresh to the back door on a daily basis. We inherited the 'mushroom man' when we took over the premises some nine years ago and he has become a good friend over the years. He used also to bring us wonderful tomatoes, courgettes and peppers which he grew, but, sadly, his glasshouses were destroyed in the hurricane. The beef recipe was included because we think our butcher is the best in the world for fillet steak and thirty minutes in the Aga with ten minutes to rest cooks his beef to perfection. The Old English Trifle is an old favourite from when we ran Chalcots Bistro in Primrose Hill. We do not grow our own produce (save the herbs) since the deer from the forest wander freely throughout the gardens and eat everything in sight.

BRAZIL NUT CRUMBLE WITH HOT CHILLI TOPPING

Serves 4

FOR THE CRUMBLE BASE

2 oz (50g) Brazil nuts, coarsely chopped
2 oz (50g) Cheddar cheese, grated
3 oz (75g) fresh wholemeal breadcrumbs
1½ tablespoons oil

FOR THE CHILLI TOPPING

8 oz (225g) mushrooms, cleaned and thinly sliced
2 oz (50g) butter
1 clove garlic, crushed
1 small onion, very finely chopped

½ teaspoon hot chilli powder,
dissolved in 2 fl oz (50ml) red wine
12 oz (350g) haricot beans, cooked and mashed
black pepper
lollo rosso leaves
chopped parsley, to garnish

Mix the Brazil nuts with the cheese and breadcrumbs, then mix in the oil to make a crumble mixture. Oil a square baking dish and press the mixture over the base. Bake for about 15 minutes in a preheated oven 375°F/190°C/Gas 5 until golden brown.

Cook the mushrooms quickly in the butter, then add all the other ingredients and cook for about 15 minutes, stirring. Season with freshly ground black pepper if desired and pour the mixture over the base. Bake for 15 minutes at the same oven temperature until cooked through.

Arrange well washed and dried lollo rosso leaves on individual plates and place squares of crumble in the middle. Sprinkle with chopped parsley and serve.

ROAST FILLET OF BEEF ON A BED OF SPICED AUBERGINES

Serves 4

olive oil
1 large onion, chopped
1 clove garlic, crushed
2 aubergines, diced, salted and well drained
large pinch each allspice, cinnamon, ginger, soft brown sugar
1 tablespoon tomato purée
8 well flavoured ripe tomatoes, peeled, deseeded and chopped
2½ lbs (1.15kg) fillet of beef, well trimmed
parsley to garnish

Sauté the onion and garlic in 3 tablespoons olive oil in a heavy based pan until soft. Add the aubergines and sauté quickly, tossing well. Add the spices and sugar and cook for 2 – 3 minutes, then add the tomato purée and chopped tomatoes. Cook on a low heat for about 1 hour.

Place the fillet in a roasting dish in a hot oven – 450°F/230°C/Gas 8 for 30 minutes (for rare meat). Allow to stand for 10 minutes, then place on a serving dish and surround with the spiced aubergines. Garnish with sprigs of parsley. Serve with leeks baked in custard, tiny new potatoes boiled in their skins and a watercress salad.

OLD ENGLISH TRIFLE

Serves 4

8 sponge fingers
2 almond macaroons
5 tablespoons Amontillado sherry
handful crushed hazelnuts, plus extra to decorate
½ pint (275ml) double cream
½ pint (275ml) milk
4 egg yolks
2 tablespoons caster sugar
4 drops vanilla essence
½ tablespoon cornflour
double cream to decorate

Break up the sponge fingers on the bottom of a glass serving dish. Crumble over the almond macaroons and moisten with the sherry. Then sprinkle over a handful of crushed hazelnuts.

Place the double cream and milk in a double boiler and bring to scalding point. Meanwhile place the egg yolks in a mixing bowl with the sugar, vanilla essence and the cornflour and mix well. Add the milk and cream mixture and stir, then pour back into the double boiler and stir over nearly boiling water until the mixture thickens. Do not allow to boil.

Strain the mixture and when slightly cooled, pour over the base and allow to cool for several hours. Decorate with whipped cream and chopped hazelnuts.

Carole Scott

THE RIVER HOUSE · THORNTON-LE-FYLDE

I came to The River House in 1982, though it had been in my husband's family since 1958. We strive to maintain an informal atmosphere for our wide spectrum of customers, with the quality of the food and cellar of the utmost importance. I enjoy researching into unusual recipes, one of the results of this has been the fillets of beef which a friend smokes in his 1930s smokehouse, as he does our salmon. We are lucky in being near to excellent suppliers of fresh fish – Dover sole, monkfish and salmon we buy from Ray Cox on the dock at Fleetwood, fresh lobster from Neve's, grouse as well as fish from Conder Fisheries and scallops, which we pick out after they have been cut, from AMC Foods. We have countless other wonderful suppliers, too numerous to mention here.

SASHIMI

*3 oz (75g) prime fillet of raw fish
(preferably salmon or tuna) per person*

FOR THE DIP
*soya sauce
Wasabi paste
garlic
sugar*

salad and sake, to serve

The secret of Sashimi is that all the ingredients must be the best and the freshest. For European taste it is best to use oily fish like salmon or tuna (preferably blue fin, yellow fin or red eye). White fish has a disagreeable texture in the mouth.

Skin, bone and fillet the fish and cut into bite-sized cubes – a friendly fishmonger given prior warning would do this for you. Make the dip by mixing all the ingredients to your individual taste.

Serve the fish on a prettily-arranged salad with tiny bowls of the dip to accompany. To eat, use Japanese pointed chopsticks to pick up the cubes of fish and place in the dip. Serve with warmed sake.

LAMB EN CROÛTE

Serves 4

*4 small pieces lamb fillet or eye of the loin
12 sheets filo pastry
4 oz (125g) butter*

FOR THE TARRAGON MOUSSE

7 oz (200g) chicken breasts
pinch mace
pinch salt
1 egg
8 fl oz (225ml) double cream
1 tablespoon chopped tarragon

FOR THE GARLIC CREAM SAUCE

8 large cloves garlic
4 fl oz (125ml) lamb stock
½ pint (275ml) double cream
dash brandy
salt

First make the tarragon mousse. Put the chicken, mace and salt in a food processor and process for 1 minute. Add the egg and mix for a further minute. Adjust seasoning. Pass through a sieve and add the chopped tarragon.

Melt the butter in a pan until you have a clear yellow liquid with bits in it. Decant off the oily part, leaving the bits in the bottom of the pan – you now have clarified butter. Pour this into a frying pan and heat until the liquid becomes clear and very hot – seal the pieces of meat until a middle brown colour.

Spread out on top of each other, on a cold surface, 3 sheets of filo pastry. Brush the top piece with melted butter. Spread a layer of tarragon mousse over the middle of the pastry, with the lamb on top. Roll up the filo pastry so that you have a little parcel. Seal the ends by pressing flat up to the edge of the contents, and cut off the flat ends. Repeat the process with each piece of lamb.

Place the parcels on a baking tray and brush the surfaces with butter. Bake in a hot oven for 12 minutes.

To make the sauce, peel and roughly chop the garlic and place in a saucepan with the lamb stock, cream and brandy. Boil until you have a thick, unctuous, garlicky cream sauce. Add salt to taste.

HONEY WAFERS

Serves 4 – 6

FOR THE WAFERS

2 oz (50g) soft butter
3 oz (75g) icing sugar
3 oz (75g) plain flour
1 egg white
3 tablespoons runny honey

FOR THE COULIS

8 oz (225g) raspberries or strawberries
3 oz (75g) icing sugar
juice of half a lemon

FOR THE CRÈME CHANTILLY

1 pint (570ml) double cream
4 oz (125g) caster sugar
1 teaspoon vanilla essence

fresh strawberries
icing sugar, to decorate

Set the oven to 350°F/180°C/Gas 4. Beat the butter, sift in the flour and sugar and beat until smooth. Add the egg white and honey and beat again. Draw circles of about 2 inches (5cm) on baking parchment and place on a greased baking tray. Take 2 teaspoons of the mixture and spread it out to fill the circle shape. Bake in the oven for 7–10 minutes until lightly browned. When cool, carefully lift on to a cooling rack. You need 3 wafers for each portion.

Place all the ingredients for the coulis in a food processor and process until smooth. Sieve.

Whip together all the ingredients for the Crème Chantilly until thick.

To assemble, pour the coulis on to plates with a wafer on top. Pipe the cream on top, add a layer of sliced strawberries and repeat until all the wafers are used up. Dust with icing sugar and decorate with a fresh strawberry.

Anna Smith

DANESCOMBE VALLEY HOTEL · CALSTOCK

The style of our cooking has been heavily influenced by our geographic position, as our raw ingredients are, almost exclusively, purchased direct by us from small individual and mostly local producers. This approach proved necessary as we are too remote from markets and specialist food shops to make anything other than an occasional foray practical; however, what at first seemed to be a problem quickly proved to hold many advantages, not least in terms of quality and freshness. The ultimate in terms of satisfaction would be to keep our own bees, rear our own poultry, make the cheeses, grow all the vegetables and perhaps even catch the salmon; however this is somewhat impractical whilst still running a busy hotel. We do, however, derive considerable enjoyment from meeting those who produce for us, and in a wider context we consider that we have a responsibility to help sustain the local economy.

BAKED GOATS CHEESE

Serves 4

4 small goat's cheeses (see below)
olive oil
Parmesan, finely grated
breadcrumbs
thyme

We use a soft goat's cheese produced by Robin Congden of Sharpham in Devon. It is about 2 inches in diameter and ¾ inch thick. We like these cheeses young and usually collect them just four days after making. As we take about forty at a time, we store those not used straight away in olive oil; this slows further maturation.

Dip each fresh goat's cheese in olive oil, then coat well in a mixture of one part finely grated Parmesan, two parts breadcrumbs and a little thyme. Bake for 10 minutes at 400°F/200°C/Gas 6 until the breadcrumbs are golden brown and the cheese heated through. Serve with a salad dressed with walnut oil.

SALMON IN AN ENVELOPE OF PAPER

Serves 4

FOR THE VEGETABLE JULIENNE

5 oz (150g) carrots
5 oz (150g) button mushrooms
5 oz (150g) onions
2 oz (50g) butter
level teaspoon chopped tarragon

4 tablespoons olive oil
2 lbs (900g) salmon, skinned and boned
salt and pepper
1 shallot, chopped
12 tarragon leaves
3 oz (75g) softened butter
8 tablespoons dry white wine
4 tablespoons chicken stock

The salmon is netted within sight of the hotel by Viv Nelson who 'shoots' from the Devon bank of the Tamar opposite Cotehele Quay. His family have been netsmen on the Tamar since the last century. There are fifteen salmon boats on the river, each boat having a licensee and a crew of two.

Cut the carrots, mushrooms and onions into julienne strips, keeping them separate.

Heat the butter in a saucepan and soften the vegetables without browning – first the carrots, then the onions, then after 5 minutes, the mushrooms. Cook together for a further 3 minutes. Stir carefully to prevent the vegetables sticking. Season and add the tarragon. Cover and continue cooking for 2 minutes. Remove from the heat and allow to cool.

Preheat the oven to 475°F/240°C/Gas 9. Cut 4 sheets of greaseproof paper into circles 14 inches (35cm) in diameter. Brush these with oil and fold into two. Open up sufficiently to pile a quarter of the vegetables julienne on to the lower half-moon of each.

Remove all the little bones from the salmon with tweezers and carve the salmon into 12 x ½ inch (1cm) slices. Lay 3 slices on top of the julienne and season with salt, pepper and chopped shallots. Add 3 tarragon leaves, 2 tablespoons wine, 1 tablespoon stock to each envelope and dot with butter.

Seal the envelopes by turning over the edges twice. Brush a roasting dish with oil and heat in the hot oven for 5 minutes. Put in the envelopes and cook for approximately 5 minutes.

Serve with new potatoes – preferably ones that have been dug that day!

LIGHT APPLE TARTS WITH HONEY ICE CREAM

Serves 4

FOR THE APPLE TARTS

8 Russet apples, peeled, cored and sliced
juice of 1 lemon
½ lb (225g) flaky pastry
4 oz (125g) butter
4 oz (125g) caster sugar

FOR THE HONEY ICE CREAM

½ pint (275ml) milk
4½ oz (140g) clear honey
2 egg yolks
½ pint (275ml) double cream

Viv Nelson, the salmon fisherman, is also one of our local beekeepers and keeps us well supplied with honey.

Place the apple slices in a bowl; sprinkle with lemon juice and mix well. Roll out the pastry very thinly; use an inverted saucer as a template to cut out 4 discs. Place the pastry on a wet baking sheet. Using a knife, draw a circle ½ inch (1cm) from the perimeter of each pastry disc and arrange the apples within this line. Dot with butter and sprinkle with caster sugar. Bake for 30 minutes in a preheated oven 425°F/220°C/Gas 7. Half way through the cooking time dot with the remaining butter and sprinkle on the remaining sugar.

Bring the milk to the boil and add the honey, whisking well. Bring back to the boil.

Put the egg yolks and cream in a large bowl and whisk until well mixed. Add the boiling milk and honey mixture and allow to cool – then empty into an electric ice-cream maker until set. Alternatively it can be placed in a plastic container in the freezer.

Kay Smith

THE WHITE HOUSE HOTEL AND RESTAURANT
WILLITON

I came with my ex-musician husband, Dick, as refugees to drowsy Somerset in the late sixties; we started the White House as enthusiastic amateurs. Originally devotees of Elizabeth David and Jane Grigson, we pursued this style of cooking, broadened it with our own ideas and inspiration from many other restaurants here and abroad, to end up running our now highly acclaimed restaurant and hotel. Our emphasis is on freshly prepared local produce.

LOVAGE SOUP

Serves 4 – 6

1 large onion, sliced
1 clove garlic, crushed
1 oz (25g) butter
2 potatoes, sliced
seasoning
1½ pints (900ml) chicken stock
2 tablespoons chopped fresh lovage
chopped parsley

The herb lovage has been grown in England since the Middle Ages, often being used as a love potion, but also to aid digestion. It flourishes in the garden without much care or attention and makes a delicious, unusual and inexpensive soup, reminiscent of celery in flavour.

Gently sauté the onion and garlic in the butter; add the potatoes and seasoning and cook for a few minutes.

Add the chicken stock and simmer for 20 minutes. Then add the lovage and simmer for a further 10 minutes. Pass through a sieve or purée in a blender. Reheat, adjust the seasoning to taste and serve sprinkled with parsley.

GRESSINGHAM DUCK WITH CARAMELISED APPLES

Serves 4

2 x 2½ – 3 lbs (1.15 – 1.4kg) ducks
a little stock
2 sharp, crisp apples
2 – 3 oz (50 – 75g) butter
2 oz (50g) sugar
watercress, to garnish

Gressingham Duck is a recently introduced hybrid based on the wild mallard, originally raised in Lancashire but franchised to various farmers throughout the country; we are fortunate in having a local supplier. It is a small, lean bird, traditionally reared, quite unlike the fatty Aylesbury duck, with quite a high proportion of breast meat and an extremely good flavour. We cook in an Aga which is ideal for this dish, but I have given approximate oven temperatures.

Prick the duck all over and season. Place on a rack in a roasting tin for ½ hour at 425°F/220°C/Gas 7. Turn upside down for a further hour at 375°F/190°C/Gas 5. Increase the heat and turn right side up for 5 – 10 minutes to crispen the skin and render away any fat under the skin, which is the most succulent and delicious part of the duck. Drain the fat and use the remaining meat juices with a little stock to moisten the meat when serving. We carve the breast meat and serve it with a leg, garnished with watercress and the caramelised apples.

Peel and core the apples and cut them into segments. To caramelise them, melt the butter, then add the sugar so that the mixture colours. Add the apple segments to the pan. Cook rapidly, turning constantly, until they are well coated and a nice golden brown. They do not need to be cooked through, but should retain a good 'bite'.

SUMMER PANCAKES

Serves 4 – 6

FOR THE PANCAKES
2 oz (50g) plain flour
1 oz (25g) buckwheat flour
1 large egg
butter, for frying
5 fl oz (150ml) milk
3 fl oz (75ml) water

about 1 lb (450g) fresh soft fruits, ideally a mixture of raspberries, loganberries, redcurrants and blackcurrants
caster sugar to taste
thick or whipped cream with natural yoghurt folded in, to serve

This is a lovely summer dish when there is a glut of soft fruits, a refreshing change to Summer Pudding. The secret is to keep the pancakes light and the fruit scarcely cooked.

Make a basic batter mix, the consistency of pouring cream. Heat some butter in a 7 inch (18cm) fryng pan – when hot pour in enough batter to thinly coat the pan (but substantial enough to turn). Cook until crisp and golden on both sides. These can be kept in a pile, covered, in a warm oven.

Put the fruit in a pan with the caster sugar and heat very gently so that the sugar melts and the juices begin to run but the fruit remains intact and just warm.

To serve, place one pancake flat on a warmed plate with a generous spoonful of the mixed fruit on top. Serve a dish of the yoghurt and cream mixture separately.

Shirley Spear

The biggest advantage of running a restaurant in Skye is the abundant supply of truly fresh shellfish, caught in the cold clear waters round the rocky shores of the Hebridean islands. Skye shellfish is the best in the world; lobster, langoustines, oysters, crab, scallops and mussels are all served in the restaurant. Fresh wild Skye salmon is one of the most popular fish dishes on the menu during the summer months, closely followed by the halibut dish given below. Fresh Scottish meat and game supplies have a little further to come, from a butcher near Inverness. A wholesaler on the island makes regular trips to Glasgow's fruit and vegetable market, although we are able to take advantage of all that is grown locally, particularly soft fruits in summertime. Supplies are a lot easier to come by than they were when we first arrived in Skye in 1984. In those days it was even difficult to obtain a regular delivery of fresh milk and cream and we found ourselves resorting to 'longlife' on many occasions during those first hard-fought months.

PAN-FRIED SCALLOPS AND BACON

Serves 4

8 fresh scallops in their shells
4 rashers bacon
2 oz (50g) butter
4 spring onions, finely chopped
(including bright green tops)
juice of 1 large orange plus a little of the zest,
mixed with 4 teaspoons whisky
assorted salad leaves (no need to dress these)

Traditionally, local scallops would have been pan-fried in fresh, homemade butter over the open fire. This dish is a modern adaptation of an old Hebridean idea. It takes only a minute or two to cook and must be served immediately, so have all the ingredients prepared beforehand. The bottom half of each scallop shell can be cleaned and used to serve this dish.

Carefully remove the scallops from their shells, discard the membrane and black intestine. Separate the pink corals. Slice the white scallop flesh through the centre horizontally.

Grill the bacon until just beginning to crisp, drain on kitchen paper, allow to cool and snip into small pieces. Melt the butter in a medium size heavy-bottomed frying pan. Toss the bacon and spring onion in the hot butter for a few seconds. Add the white scallop meat and fry gently until just turning opaque. Add the corals for a few seconds more.

Pour over the orange and whisky mixture quickly but gently and combine all the ingredients together until the liquid is just warmed through.

Have ready the scallop shells, each arranged on a bed of pretty salad leaves. Divide the scallops evenly between the four shells and spoon over the warm pan juices. Serve immediately with thin slices of wholemeal bread and butter to soak up the juices.

BAKED HALIBUT FILLET WITH STRAWBERRY AND BLACK PEPPERCORN SAUCE

Serves 4

few thin lemon slices
1 sprig parsley with good piece of stalk
1 small bay leaf
4 x 6 oz (175g) pieces halibut fillet
pinch sea salt
dry white wine
1 oz (25g) butter

FOR THE SAUCE

1 lb (450g) fresh strawberries
(not over-ripe or the finished sauce will taste fusty)
1 teaspoon finely chopped fresh mint,
plus extra mint leaves
juice and finely grated zest of 1 small lemon
1 level tablespoon caster sugar
freshly ground black pepper

Scotland is famous for its soft summer fruits. Some Scotsmen say that the best and only way to sample the first pick of the new crop of strawberries is with a liberal sprinkling of freshly ground black pepper – an idea which I have adapted here with great success – it is one of the most popular dishes in the restaurant.

Preheat the oven to 375°F/190°C/Gas 5. Place 2 or 3 thin slices of lemon, the parsley and bay leaf in an ovenproof dish large enough to take the pieces of fish. Place the fish in the dish, spaced slightly apart. Season very lightly with sea salt and pour a dash of white wine over each piece.

Cover completely with a sheet of lightly buttered greaseproof paper. Seal the dish with kitchen foil or a tight fitting lid and cook in the centre of the oven for 15–20 minutes depending on the thickness of the fillets.

Prepare the strawberries in the usual way. Reserve 4 good heart-shaped ones for garnish. Place the strawberries with all the other ingredients except the black pepper in a food processor and purée. Rub the purée through a nylon sieve to obtain a smooth sauce. Check that the sauce tastes sharp but not too acidic and add a fraction more sugar if necessary.

Just before serving, heat the sauce thoroughly, then add a liberal amount of black pepper straight from the mill and stir it in quickly. Pour a pool of the sauce straightaway on to warmed dinner plates. Lift the fillets carefully on to the sauce. (Reserve the cooking juices for another sauce or fish stock). Garnish each one with a thinly sliced fan of fresh strawberry and a small mint leaf. Serve immediately with baby new potatoes and a lightly cooked green vegetable such as sprigs of broccoli or mange-tout.

THREE CHIMNEYS HOT MARMALADE PUDDING

Serves 4

5 oz (150g) fresh brown breadcrumbs
4 oz (125g) soft light brown sugar
1 oz (25g) self-raising wholemeal flour
4 oz (125g) butter, plus extra for greasing
8 tablespoons strong flavoured coarse-cut marmalade
3 large eggs
1 rounded teaspoon bicarbonate of soda

This steamed pudding is immensely light with a deep tangy flavour. It is not, as some people imagine, a stodgy suet pudding with a dollop of marmalade at the bottom of the basin. The marmalade is combined throughout, giving the finished dessert a rich amber colour. It is so popular that it has never been off the menu – the secret lies in my homemade coarse-cut marmalade of which I make hundreds of pounds every winter.

Butter a 2 pint (1.1 litre) pudding basin.

Place the breadcrumbs, flour and sugar in a large mixing bowl. Melt the butter and marmalade together in a saucepan over a gentle heat and pour over the dry ingredients. Mix well together. Whisk the eggs and blend them in thoroughly. Dissolve the bicarbonate of soda in 1 tablespoon of cold water. Stir into the pudding mixture and pour into the prepared basin.

Cover the top of the basin with a circle of buttered greaseproof paper, followed by a circle of kitchen foil. Both should be pleated across the centre to allow room for expansion. Tie them on securely with string around the edge of the basin. Place the pudding in a saucepan of boiling water so that the water comes half-way up the side of the basin. Cover the saucepan with a well-fitting lid and simmer the pudding for 2 hours, keeping the water topped up at all times. Turn out on to a serving dish and serve hot with whipped cream.

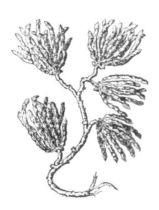

Kate Taylor

*The stalls in the covered hall of Swansea market have little in common with
the shelves of city supermarkets where most of us modern Brits now shop.
Vegetable stalls are piled high with garden greenery; fish are glistening and
still moving, fresh from the landing that day; Welsh cheeses nestle alongside
a cornucopia of the best of the French; cockles and laverbread have come from
the lovely old ladies of the Gower peninsula along with home-reared chicks
and ducks; Welsh cakes are hot from the griddle – one could graze well here.
The restaurant does well too, with fresh ingredients guaranteed and menu-
planning largely a matter of glorious chance. By buying well, cooking
simply and seasonally, the chef cannot go far wrong!*

RILLETTES OF DUCK

Serves 8

1 small duck, about 1 lb (450g)
1 lb (450g) belly pork, without skin or bone
1 small glass dry white wine
good teaspoon dried thyme or several sprigs fresh
salt and freshly ground black pepper
freshly grated nutmeg
2 bay leaves
1 onion, chopped
1 carrot, chopped
1 stick celery, chopped
½ tablespoon green peppercorns in brine
1 tablespoon chopped parsley
watercress, lettuce and gherkins, for garnish

Cut the duck, including bones, into 2 inch
(5cm) pieces using a cleaver or heavy knife. Cut
the pork into 1 inch (2.5cm) dice. Place the meat
in an ovenproof dish with all the other
ingredients except the peppercorns and
parsley. Cover tightly with foil and cook in a low
oven 300°F/150°C/Gas 2 for 2 hours or until very
tender.

Remove from the oven and cool in a metal
colander, reserving the juices. While still warm,
remove the duck skin and bones and
vegetables and discard. Shred the meat by
hand or using 2 forks. Mix well and add more
salt and pepper until you have a fairly highly-
seasoned mixture.

Add the green peppercorns and parsley if
using and pack the meat loosely into ramekins,
leaving a ½ inch (1 cm) gap at the top. Pour over
the reserved juices to cover, then allow to cool,
cover with clingfilm and refrigerate until set.

Remove from the refrigerator 1 hour before
serving. Unmould on to plates and garnish
with watercress, lettuce and gherkins. Serve
with French bread and a good vinaigrette. The
rillettes will keep for several days in the
refrigerator.

SAUTÉ OF CHICKEN WITH WATERCHESTNUTS

Serves 8

vegetable oil
8 breasts of chicken, skinned and cut into strips
1 heaped tablespoon finely chopped fresh ginger
1 red pepper, seeded and cut into thin strips
1 green pepper, seeded and cut into thin strips
1 tablespoon dry or medium sherry
soy sauce
salt and freshly ground black pepper
2 x 8 oz (225g) tins waterchestnuts
¾ pint (400ml) single cream

Heat 1 – 2 tablespoons oil in a large, heavy frying pan over a high heat. Brown the strips of chicken quickly in the oil. Add the ginger, then lower the heat and add the peppers. Fry gently for a few minutes until the chicken is firm. Add the sherry, a sprinkling of soy sauce and salt and pepper. Add the waterchestnuts with all their juices. Allow to bubble for a few minutes, remove from the heat and add the cream. Warm through again, shaking the pan to amalgamate the cream into the sauce. Do not boil too vigorously or the sauce will separate. Place in a warmed dish, sprinkle with chives and serve immediately with plain Basmati rice.

STRAWBERRIES CHANTILLY

Serves 8

FOR THE MACAROONS
6 oz (175g) ground almonds
6 oz (175g) icing sugar, plus extra for sprinkling
½ cap vanilla essence
2 egg whites

2 lbs (900g) fresh strawberries
1 lb (450g) fresh or frozen raspberries
caster sugar
½ pint (275ml) double cream

First make the macaroons. Mix the ground almonds and icing sugar thoroughly in a bowl, add the vanilla essence and gradually mix in the egg whites to form a dough. It should not be too sticky. Make small balls of dough and flatten them slightly. Place on a baking sheet covered with a sheet of greaseproof paper. Moisten the tops with a pastry brush dipped in water and sprinkle with icing sugar. Bake at 400 – 425°F/200 – 220°C/Gas 6 – 7 for 10 – 15 minutes until lightly browned.

Immediately after removing from the oven, lift a corner of the greaseproof paper and tip 1 tablespoon water underneath. The steam will loosen the macaroons which can be lifted with a palette knife and place on a rack to cool.

Hull the strawberries and divide between 8 sundae dishes or small glass bowls. Liquidise the raspberries with sugar to taste. Sieve the purée and spoon it over the strawberries. Whip the cream until thick and sweeten to taste. Pipe the cream over the strawberries and garnish with the macaroons. Serve cold.

Carol Trevor-Roper

BROOKDALE HOUSE · NORTH HUISH

Although I have now 'retired' from the kitchen at Brookdale, I am still actively involved in the hotel. As far as possible the ingredients we use are local, additive free and many are organically produced. Ben Watson at Riverford Farm rears pigs on natural diets and produces excellent pork, ham, bacon and sausages. Ben also provides us with chickens, again fed a natural diet, well hung Devon beef and lamb reared on organic pastures. Peter Hayford from Lower Bearscombe Farm provides us with free range quail, guinea fowl, Aylesbury and cross-bred ducks as well as quail eggs. Mark Lobb from Stoke Fleming supplies game in season and all our fish from the Brixham Fish Cooperative. We also purchase meat from Chris McCabe in Totnes who sells guaranteed additive free meat. Charles Staniland from Buckland in the Moor grows us herbs, specialist vegetables and delicious strawberries in his organic garden. We also buy vegetables and fruit from Challices in Totnes. We use traditionally produced cream from Langage Farm as well as free range eggs. Ticklemore Cheese Shop in Totnes supplies us with excellent unpasteurised cheeses. This buying policy ensures the highest quality of ingredients as well as a diet free from all chemical food additives.

SALCOMBE CRAB TARTLETS

Serves 4

FOR THE PASTRY BASE

4 oz (125g) flour
½ teaspoon salt
2 oz (50g) butter
½ teaspoon salt
1 oz (25g) crushed walnuts
1 egg yolk
2 tablespoons cold water

8 oz (225g) brown crabmeat
2 tomatoes, peeled, deseeded and diced
4 spring onions, finely chopped

½ teaspoon English mustard
salt and black pepper to taste
8 oz (225g) white crabmeat
juice and zest of 1 lime
1 teaspoon finely chopped ginger

FOR THE HOLLANDAISE SAUCE

1 tablespoon lemon juice
2 egg yolks
4 oz (125g) unsalted butter, cubed
1 heaped tablespoon finely chopped fresh basil
salt and pepper to taste

Sift the flour and salt into a food processor. Dice the butter into small cubes and add to the flour with the crushed walnuts. Beat the egg yolk and water together and process all the ingredients together for no more than 30 seconds. Turn out on to a lightly floured board and knead the dough to a ball. Wrap in clingfilm and refrigerate for at least 30 minutes.

Butter 4 x 4 inch (10cm) tartlet tins. Roll out the pastry and line the tins, pricking the bases thoroughly with a fork. Chill again for at least 15 minutes. Bake blind in a pre-heated oven 400°F/200°C/Gas 6 for 6 – 10 minutes, then bake uncovered for a further 5 minutes. Cool, remove carefully from the tins and transfer to a rack.

Mix together the brown crabmeat, tomatoes, spring onions, and mustard. Season to taste and refrigerate until needed.

Mix together the white crabmeat with the lime juice and zest, and the fresh ginger; season to taste and refrigerate.

To make the Hollandaise sauce, bring a pan of water to simmering point. Beat the egg yolks and lemon juice together in a glass or stainless steel bowl and place over the pan. Add the cubes of butter gradually, stirring all the time, until all the butter is used and the sauce is smooth and fairly thick. Remove from the heat and gently stir in the chopped basil. Season to taste and keep warm.

To assemble, fill each tartlet with a layer of brown, then a layer of white crabmeat. Top each with a generous spoonful of Hollandaise and glaze quickly under a pre-heated grill. Serve immediately.

SPINACH STUFFED RIVERFORD PORK WITH APRICOT AND KUMMEL SAUCE

Serves 4

1½ lbs (700g) pork tenderloin
1 lb (450g) spinach
3 oz (75g) butter
½ teaspoon grated nutmeg
2 shallots, finely chopped
1 tablespoon water
1 tablespoon soy sauce

FOR THE SAUCE

1 lb (450g) fresh apricots, stoned
1 tablespoon brown sugar
juice of 1 lemon
1 tablespoon water
1 teaspoon allspice
1 tablespoon Kummel

Trim the fat from the tenderloin and remove the transparent skin. Slit the meat lengthways through half its thickness and flatten it out.

Wash and blanch the spinach, drain and chop it finely. Melt 1 oz (25g) butter in a pan, add the shallots and cook until softened. Add the spinach and nutmeg and season to taste. Spread the spinach over the tenderloin, roll up tightly and tie up with string.

Melt the remaining butter in a flameproof dish and fry the meat until evenly browned. Mix the water and soy sauce together and pour over the pork. Cover the pan tightly with a lid and cook in the oven for 45 minutes at 325°F/170°C/Gas 3. Remove the lid, baste the pork and cook for a further 15 minutes uncovered.

To make the sauce, place all the ingredients except the Kummel in a pan. Cook for about 5 – 10 minutes, stirring often until the apricots are soft. Cool slightly then liquidise in a blender and pass through a sieve. Add the Kummel and season to taste.

Reheat the sauce, remove the string from the pork and slice. Arrange on serving plates and spoon the sauce around. Serve with new potatoes and new baby carrots.

MERINGUE TIMBALES WITH STRAWBERRIES IN GRENADINE

Serves 4

½ oz (10g) butter
4 egg whites
4 oz (125g) caster sugar
1 teaspoon vanilla essence
12 oz (350g) strawberries
½ pint (275ml) Grenadine syrup
5 fl oz (150ml) double cream, lightly whipped

Butter 4 x 3½ inch (8.5cm) diameter ramekin dishes or large teacups and refrigerate them.

Whisk the egg whites until stiff and add the sugar and vanilla essence. Whisk again until firm. Fill the prepared moulds, leaving an inch headspace and place in a baking tin half-filled with water. Cover with wetted greaseproof paper and cook in the oven at 325°F/170°C/Gas 3 for 20–25 minutes until risen and firm to touch. Leave to cool and turn out on to a damp tea towel.

Wipe, hull and quarter the strawberries. pour over the Grenadine syrup and chill for at least 1 hour.

To assemble, place the meringue on a serving plate, coat with the cream and surround with the strawberries.

Pauline Whittaker

Country Friends is housed in a Salopian black and white building dating back to 1670. The restaurant seats 40 and there are three bedrooms for those guests who over-indulge! Over the last six years we have built up an interesting array of suppliers from within the county, from farmhouse butter and cheeses to locally farmed venison, all leading to the fresh tastes which we regard as our strength.

SALMON BRANDADE

Serves 8

1 lb (450g) fresh salmon
2 fl oz (50ml) olive oil
juice of 2 lemons
1 clove garlic, crushed
freshly ground black pepper
2 tablespoons breadcrumbs
5 fl oz (150ml) cream

Chop the salmon into 1 inch (2.5cm) cubes and cook in the olive oil together with the lemon juice and crushed garlic for 10 minutes.

Remove from the heat and add the black pepper, breadcrumbs and cream. Beat all the ingredients well together, then transfer the mixture to a 2 lb (900g) loaf tin.

Bake in a bain-marie at 375°F/190°C/Gas 5 for 20 minutes. Remove from the oven, allow to cool and chill in the refrigerator. Serve in slices with a salad and hot toast, or, even better, toasted brioche.

CHICKEN BREASTS IN PUFF PASTRY

Serves 4

6 oz (175g) cream cheese
handful mixed chopped fresh herbs
1 clove garlic, chopped (optional)
4 boned chicken breasts, skinned

FOR THE PASTRY

4 oz (125g) butter
4 oz (125g) lard
8 oz (225g) flour
squeeze lemon juice
water
1 beaten egg

Mix the cream cheese with the herbs and garlic, if used. Beat well. Pipe the mixture into the flap of each chicken breast and set aside.

To make the pastry, cut the butter and lard into the flour. Mix lightly with water and a squeeze of lemon juice. Turn on to a floured surface, roll lightly into an oblong shape and fold into three. Repeat the process about 6 times until the pastry is smooth.

Roll out the pastry and cut out 4 large circles. Wrap up each chicken breast carefully in a pastry circle, making sure the parcel is well sealed. Brush with the beaten egg and place on a baking tray. Bake for 30 minutes at 425°F/220°C/Gas 7.

There is no need for a sauce with this dish as the melted cheese will flood out as you cut into the parcel.

CHOCOLATE ROULADE

Serves 8

6 oz (175g) plain chocolate
3 tablespoons water
5 eggs, separated
5 oz (150g) caster sugar
whipping cream and fresh fruit, for filling
(raspberries or black cherries)

Melt the chocolate and beat in the water.

Whisk together the egg yolks and the sugar, then gradually beat in the chocolate.

Beat the egg whites until stiff and fold them carefully into the mixture. Pour into a greased and lined Swiss roll tin and bake for 12 minutes at 400°F/200°C/Gas 6. Cover with greaseproof paper and a damp tea towel. When cold, fill with whipped cream and fresh fruit and roll up carefully.

Joanna Wickens

WICKENS · NORTHLEACH

Our recently-extended restaurant is housed in a Cotswold stone building in Northleach market square. We believe in using the very best and freshest local ingredients, cooked so that the original flavour stands out. We specialise in English cuisine – lamb from a local producer is always favourite – indeed we try to buy local produce whenever possible. We have an unusual wine list with wines solely from English-speaking producers – Australia, New Zealand, California, Washington State, Idaho and England. We like to serve fine local cheeses such as single Gloucester with nettles to finish the meal.

BLACK PUDDING SALAD

Serves 4

2 rashers bacon, diced
1 small round of black pudding, sliced
1 stick celery, finely diced
¼ red pepper, finely diced
¼ green pepper, finely diced
1 green apple, diced
mixed salad leaves, eg: lollo rosso, curly endive, radicchio, oak leaf, iceberg

FOR THE DRESSING

1 tablespoon grain mustard
juice of 1 orange
2 tablespoons wine vinegar
1 dessertspoon soft brown sugar
salt and pepper to taste
7 fl oz (200ml) good quality vegetable oil
4 fl oz (125ml) walnut oil

Blend all the ingredients for the dressing in a liquidiser, adding the oil slowly. This should make quite a thick dressing – thin down with a little more orange juice if necessary.

Quickly fry the bacon in a little oil. Add the black pudding and fry, turning once. Add the celery, peppers and apple, mixing gently, followed by the dressing to taste. Let it bubble up for a moment, then pour over the arranged salad leaves and serve immediately.

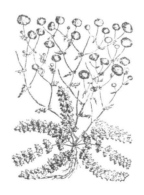

MARINATED MONKFISH AND SALMON

Serves 4

3 teaspoons cumin seeds
8 tablespoons plain yoghurt
¼ teaspoon ground ginger
1 large clove garlic, crushed
zest and juice of 1 lemon
salt and black pepper
½ teaspoon garam masala
2 oz (50g) unsalted butter
1 lb (450g) monkfish, cut into medium sized pieces
1 lb (450g) salmon, cut into medium sized pieces

Roast the cumin seeds in a small, heavy frying pan, without fat or oil, over a medium flame. Stir the seeds until they turn a few shades darker. They keep well in an airtight container.

Put the yoghurt in a bowl and add the ginger, garlic, lemon zest and juice, salt and pepper, cumin seeds and garam masala; mix well. Add the fish and coat thoroughly. Leave to marinate for 1–2 hours.

Melt the butter in a large frying pan. When completely melted, pour in the marinade and stir well until bubbling. Simmer until reduced by a third. Add the fish and cook for 3–5 minutes, stirring gently.

Serve immediately with brown rice and a crisp vegetable or a salad.

APPLE AND FRANGIPANE DUMPLINGS

Serves 6

1 lb (450g) eating apples
sugar syrup
5 oz (150g) butter or margarine
3 oz (75g) caster sugar
few drops vanilla essence
2 eggs
3 oz (75g) ground almonds
3 sheets filo pastry
icing sugar
cream, or fruit coulis, to serve

Cut up the apples into ¼ – ½ inch (0.5–1cm) dice and poach in the sugar syrup to soften slightly. Leave to cool in the liquid.

Beat 3 oz (75g) of the butter with the caster sugar until light and pale. Gradually beat in the vanilla essence, eggs and ground almonds.

Melt the remaining 2 oz (50g) butter and brush a little into 12 sections of a bun tin. Cut the filo pastry into 5 inch (12cm) squares. Keep the pastry covered with a damp teatowel until ready to use.

To make the dumplings, butter one square of pastry, place a second on top and brush with more butter. Place about 1 dessertspoon of almond mixture into the centre and top with a few pieces of apple. Gather up the edges of the pastry, folding over the filling to enclose. Turn over and shape into a neat round. Place seam-side down in the buttered tin. Repeat to make 12 dumplings.

Brush with melted butter and bake at 400°F/200°C/Gas 6 for 20 minutes. Ease out of the tin and dust with icing sugar. Serve hot with either cream or a fruit coulis. The dumplings reheat extremely well.

Shirley Wilkes

THE RIVER HOUSE · EXMOUTH

It was our pleasure in entertaining friends that first attracted Michael and me to the idea of owning our own restaurant. What we did not realise is that a business situation is quite different and the amount of work involved extremely exhausting. However, fifteen years later we still love it and strive to achieve a happy and informal atmosphere.

With the water lapping against our walls we have no garden and so, in order to grow the fresh herbs that are vital to so many of our dishes, we cultivate three allotments in the village. We also grow some of our vegetables and salads, fruit for ice creams and sorbets as well as flowers for the tables so when we are not cooking we are frantically gardening!

'Entertaining At Home' is the theme for my regular Cookery Demonstrations and the following recipes are ideas we have developed from them. They are simple to prepare and can be organised well ahead – essential to hassle free entertaining.

PAUPIETTE OF CUCUMBER AND SMOKED SALMON

Serves 6

½ cucumber, peeled, deseeded and finely diced
½ teaspoon salt
½ tablespoon tarragon vinegar
6 oz (175g) thinly sliced smoked salmon (or good smoked trout fillet)
5 fl oz (150ml) yoghurt or cream
4 oz (125g) cottage cheese
4 oz (125g) cream cheese
freshly ground white pepper
cayenne pepper
1 teaspoon chopped chives and parsley
1½ teaspoons gelatine dissolved in 2 tablespoons water
a little black lumpfish, lemon wedges, grapefruit

segments, radicchio, lambs lettuce and finely shredded Webbs lettuce to decorate

This starter has a delicious and unusual fresh taste. It also looks quite stunning – a good talking point for the beginning of a meal.

Place the cucumber with the salt and vinegar in a bowl; mix together well. Tip into a colander and leave a weighted plate on top of the cucumber for at least 30 minutes.

Line 6 individual ramekin dishes or small moulds with clingfilm and lay thin slices of smoked salmon, trimmed with scissors, in the base and around the inside of each mould.

Whiz together the yoghurt or cream and cottage cheese in a food processor until a smooth consistency, then add the cream cheese, seasonings and herbs. Whiz again and taste for flavour – you may need to add a little more cayenne and perhaps a little lemon juice. Beware of adding too much salt because of the smoked salmon.

Pat the cucumber dry and add to the mixture with the well-dissolved gelatine. Whiz briefly in the processor to mix the cucumber into the cheese mixture, then pour into the smoked salmon-lined moulds.

Turn out the mousses, with the smoked salmon on top, on to individual plates (preferably white) and decorate with a little lumpfish, salad leaves, grapefruit segments and thin wedges of lemon.

SMOKED OYSTER AND HERB STUFFED QUAIL BRAISED IN SHERRY

Serves 6

12 boned quail
4 baby leeks (or spring onions), thinly sliced
3 rashers streaky or back bacon, finely chopped and quickly fried in oil or butter
½ pint (275ml) medium sherry
½ pint (275ml) light chicken stock
salt and pepper
garden herbs (thyme, marjoram, winter savory, parsley and chives)
red lettuce and watercress, to serve

FOR THE STUFFING

1 tin smoked oysters, finely sliced
3 oz (75g) breadcrumbs, crisped in a little oil or butter
2 tablespoons finely chopped garden herbs (as above)

This is an idea collected from a holiday in Spain. You can use the quail on the bone but they are very fiddly to eat and a bit of a conversation stopper!

Mix together all the ingredients for the stuffing. Open out all the quail and put a tablespoon of stuffing inside each. Close up the quail flesh around the stuffing and secure with 2 cocktail sticks for each one.

On a bed of leeks and bacon, place the quail, breast side up, side by side in an ovenproof dish. Sprinkle with a little salt, freshly ground black pepper and a good sprinkling of garden herbs.

Heat the sherry and chicken stock together and pour over the quails. Brush the tops of the birds with a little melted butter and place the dish in a very hot oven for 5 minutes. Turn the oven down to 325°F/170°C/Gas 3.

Cover the dish with foil and return to the oven for 30 minutes or until the birds are cooked. Baste with the cooking juices at least once during the cooking time.

When cooked, pour off the juices into a shallow pan and reduce to half the quantity. At the last moment add a little unsalted butter to give the sauce a shine. If the quails look a little pale on top, they can be brushed with melted butter and finished under a hot grill for a few seconds.

Serve on an oval platter with red lettuce and watercress.

Braised Celery with Bacon and Walnuts makes a good accompaniment. Blanch and refresh the celery, add sautéed chopped spring onions, then simmer in chicken stock with a little oregano. Garnish with little pieces of crisply fried bacon, walnuts and plenty of finely chopped parsley.

PEARS POACHED IN LEMON SYRUP WITH STEM GINGER

Serves 6

¾ pint (400ml) water
12 oz (350g) caster sugar
1½ – 2 pears per person
2 thin slices lemon for each pear
about 3 chunks stem ginger (according to taste)
additional lemon and sprigs of lemon balm, to decorate
Greek yoghurt and cream, to serve

This light dessert looks very attractive and after a fairly rich main course makes a refreshing end to a meal.

Make a sugar syrup by simmering the water and sugar for 5 minutes. Peel the pears, leaving the stalks on, and either leave whole or cut in half and remove the cores.

Poach the pears in the syrup with the lemon slices until tender. This can be done either in a dish covered with clingfilm in the microwave, in a deep pan over a low heat, or in a covered casserole dish in a low oven. The cooking time will depend on the method used and the size of the pears.

Chop the ginger into very small pieces and add for the last 5 minutes of cooking time.

Serve in a glass bowl with the pears upright and pour the syrup over. Decorate with fresh twists of lemon and small sprigs of lemon balm. Greek yoghurt mixed with cream makes a wonderful accompaniment.

Alison Yetman

YETMAN'S · HOLT

*I think formal training can sometimes be as much of a hindrance as a help –
like wearing a culinary straitjacket. I look at Raymond Blanc's recipes and
am amazed by their originality, but having accepted that I will never possess
that exciting flair and inventiveness, I keep to my own style of simple,
uncluttered flavours – I don't have the time or the inclination for elaborate
garnishes and this recipe for Brioche filled with Chicken Livers is about as
complicated as I get!*

HERB BRIOCHE FILLED WITH CHICKEN LIVERS AND BACON

Serves 4

1 oz (25g) sugar
½ oz (10g) yeast
1 lb 1 oz (475g) strong plain white flour
2 teaspoons salt
3 fl oz (75ml) warm milk
6 eggs, beaten
12 oz (350g) unsalted butter, very soft
1 small bunch each tarragon, chervil, dill, finely chopped
egg yolk to glaze

FOR THE FILLING

12 oz (350g) chicken livers, fresh or frozen
*8 rashers smoked streaky bacon,
de-rinded and chopped*
salt and black pepper
2 oz (50g) butter
8 oz (225g) carton natural Greek yoghurt
small bunch chives, snipped
extra chives or chopped parsley to decorate

This quantity will make about 30 brioches; the cooked brioches or surplus dough may be frozen (see below). Vary the flavours by adding nuts or cheese instead of the herbs.

Start the dough the day before you want to use it. In a small bowl mix 1 teaspoon sugar with the yeast until liquid, add approximately 1 fl oz (25ml) warm water and leave in a warm place to froth.

Sift the flour, sugar and salt together into a large bowl. Take about 4 oz (125g) of this and whisk into the yeast mixture together with the warm milk. Cover with a polythene bag and leave to rise for about 20 – 30 minutes.

Pour the fermented dough into the remaining flour mixture and work until smooth, using your whole hand with fingers apart, adding the eggs as you go. This will leave you with a very soft, elastic dough. Gradually work the butter into the dough with your hand; this will take some time (about 15 minutes) but you should finish with a shiny, sticky dough. Incorporate the herbs, dust with flour, cover with polythene and leave in a warm place to rise for about 2 hours or until doubled in size.

Knock back by flipping the dough over a

couple of times with your fingers, dust with flour, cover with polythene and a damp cloth (this stops the dough escaping all over the fridge) and refrigerate overnight. The dough can be successfully frozen at this stage.

In the morning the dough should be risen but much firmer in texture. Leaving half the dough in the fridge so as not to soften too much, work with the remaining dough as fast as you can. Using a minimum of dusting flour, take a piece of dough the size of a mandarin orange, form two-thirds of it into a ball and place in a greased brioche tin. Make a large hole in the centre with your finger, mould the remaining third into an egg shape and insert into the hole, point downwards. Brush lightly with beaten egg yolk mixed with water. Shape the remaining dough in the same way and allow the brioches to rise for about 20 minutes. Brush lightly again and bake immediately for 8–10 minutes for 450°F/230°C/Gas 8. Cool on a wire rack.

For the filling, remove any tubes or green bile marks from the livers and cut each into 3. Fry the bacon until crisp in a little butter and keep warm. Melt about 1 oz (25g) butter in the frying pan and when hot, throw in the livers, turning briskly with a spatula, for a couple of minutes so that they remain pink in the centre. Add the cooked bacon and stir in the yoghurt and chives off the heat.

Have ready 4 hot plates and the brioches, warmed. Remove their tops with a twist, pile in the chicken livers and spoon any left-over mixture on to the plates. Replace the brioche tops or leave at the side and sprinkle with more chives or freshly chopped parsley.

BAKED HALIBUT WITH HERBS AND A FRESH TOMATO SAUCE

Serves 4

5 fl oz (150ml) extra virgin olive oil
2 fat cloves garlic, crushed
small bunch thyme and basil
4 thick halibut steaks,
cut from either side of the backbone

FOR THE SAUCE

2 lbs (900g) ripe, well-flavoured tomatoes
1 medium Spanish onion, finely chopped
1 clove garlic, crushed
2 tablespoons olive oil
salt and pepper

Heat the olive oil in a pan with the garlic, thyme and a little of the basil until bubbling. Remove from the heat and leave to infuse until cool.

To make the sauce, blanch the tomatoes in boiling water and refresh. Peel, deseed and dice them. Sweat the onions and garlic in the oil until transparent, then remove from the heat and gently stir in the tomatoes, salt and pepper.

Cut 4 large squares of foil, brush liberally with the herb-flavoured oil and place a piece of fish on each one. Brush with the remaining oil and sprinkle the remaining basil on top. Make each into a well-sealed parcel and cook on a baking sheet in the middle of a hot oven for 15 – 20 minutes or until the fish 'gives' when pressed.

Gently reheat the tomato sauce until just warm but don't allow it to go mushy. Place a large spoonful in the middle of each plate. Quickly unwrap the halibut and remove the skin, place on top of the sauce and tip any juices over. Garnish with extra herbs if you like and serve with new potatoes and a green salad.

LEMON AND ALMOND ROULADE

Serves 6 – 8

FOR THE LEMON CURD

8 oz (225g) caster sugar
4 oz (125g) unsalted butter
grated rind and juice of 3 large lemons
3 eggs

FOR THE ROULADE

4 large eggs, separated
4 oz (125g) caster sugar
grated zest and juice of 1 lemon
3 oz (75g) ground almonds
½ pint (275ml) double cream, whipped

Make the lemon curd in advance – this quantity will fill 2 roulades. Place all ingredients except the eggs in a basin fitting snugly over a saucepan of boiling water. Leave over the heat until the sugar and butter have melted completely.

Whisk the eggs in a separate bowl, then strain through a sieve into another bowl or jug. Start beating the lemon mixture and quickly pour in the eggs, beating fast until all the egg is incorporated. Cover the basin and leave to cook gently over the hot water, stirring with a whisk every few minutes. The final texture should be like half-whipped cream. Either pour into warmed jars or leave in a bowl covered with clingfilm to prevent a skin forming.

To make the roulade, put the yolks and half the sugar into a wide bowl with the lemon rind and whisk together until thickened and beginning to trail. Fold in the ground almonds and lemon juice.

Whisk the egg whites until stiff, then add the remaining sugar and whisk for another 10 seconds. Fold into the egg and almond mixture a little at a time, using a balloon whisk with quick movements, or a large metal spoon. Do not over-mix or you will lose all the air. Spread the mixture on silicone paper on a large baking sheet, about 12 inches x 18 inches (30.5 x 46cm) and bake at 325°F/170°C/Gas 3 for about 15 minutes until golden brown and springy to the touch.

Have ready a large sheet of greaseproof paper, sprinkled liberally with caster sugar. Tip the roulade on to this, paper side up, and very quickly and carefully remove the silicone paper. Do this in strips if the sponge threatens to tear or stick. Leave to cool for about 10 – 15 minutes, spread with lemon curd and whipped cream and roll up like a Swiss roll, using the paper to tilt the roulade.

Restaurant Addresses

The Women Chefs of Britain was first published in November 1990.
Since that time a few of the restaurants featured have either
closed down or changed hands, consequently we have deleted
their address details from the list below.

Airds Hotel, Port Appin, Strathclyde
01631 730236

Altnaharrie Inn, Ullapool, Highland
01854 633230

Ann Fitzgerald's Farmhouse Kitchen, Mathry,
Dyfed 01348 831347

The Ark, The Street, Erpingham, Norfolk
01263 761535

At the Sign of the Angel, Lacock, Wilts
01249730 230

Ballymaloe House, Shanagarry, Co Cork
00353 21652531

Bridgefield House, Spark Bridge, Cumbria
01229 885239

Carved Angel, Dartmouth, Devon 0180 432465

Chedington Court, Chedington, Dorset
01935 891265

Clarke's, 124 Kensington Church Street, London
0171 2219225

Cnapan, East Street, Newport, Dyfed
01239 820575

Corse Lawn House, Corse Lawn,
Gloucestershire 01452 780479

Country Friends, Dorrington, Shropshire
01743 718707

Cringletie House, Peebles, Borders
01721 730233

Cromwellian, Kirkham, Lancashire
01772 685680

The Cross, Kingussie, Highland 01540 661762

Croque-en-Bouche, Malvern Wells, Hereford &
Worcester 01684 565612

Danescombe Valley Hotel, Calstock, Cornwall
01822 832414

Gilberts, 2 Exhibition Road, London
0171 589 8947

Hope End, Ledbury, Hereford & Worcester
01531 3613

Hunts Tor House, Drewsteignton, Devon
01647 281228

Kinloch Lodge, Isle Ornsay, Sleat, Isle of Skye
01471 833333

Landgate Bistro, Rye, East Sussex 01797 222829

Langley Wood, Redlynch, Wiltshire
01794 390348

La Potiniere, Gullane, Lothian 01620 843214

Le Mesurier, 113 Old Street, London
0171 251 8117

Little Barwick House, Barwick, Yeovil, Somerset
01935 23902

Lynwood House, Barnstaple, Devon
01271 43695

The Manor, Chadlington, Oxfordshire
01608 676711

Manor House Inn, Shotley Bridge, Co Durham
01207 255268

The Marsh Goose, High Street, Moreton
01608 652111

Moorings, Wells-next-the-Sea, Norfolk
01328 710949

Old Vicarage, Ridgeway, Derbyshire
01142 475814

Polmaily House, Drumnadrochit, Highland
01456 450343

Poppies, The Roebuck, Brimfield, Hereford &
Worcester 01584 711230

River House, Lympstone, Devon 01395 265147

Seaview Hotel, Seaview, Isle of Wight
01983 612711

Three Chimneys, Dunvegan, Isle of Skye
01470 511258

Tiroran House, Tiroran, Isle of Mull
01681 705232

Village Restaurant, Ramsbottom, Greater
Manchester 0170 6825070

White House Hotel, Williton, Somerset
01984 632306

Wickens, Northleach, Gloucestershire
01451 860421

Woods, Bath, Avon 01225 314812

Y Bistro, Llanberis, Gwynedd 01286 871278

Yetmans, Holt, Norfolk 01263 713320

Index